John,

financial advisor,
It's all of true
with him!

Meet Me on Friday Morning

OUR LIFE AND WORK TOGETHER

Chris White and Suzanne White

All Scripture quotations, unless otherwise indicated, are taken from the *Holy Bible, New International Version*®, NIV®. Copyright ©1973, 1978, 1984, 2011 by Biblica Inc.® Used by permission. All rights reserved worldwide. Scripture quotations marked (KJV) are taken from the King James Version. Scripture quotations marked (TLB) are taken from *The Living Bible* Copyright ©1971. Used by permission of Tyndale House Publishers Inc., Carol Stream, Illinois 60188. All rights reserved.

ISBN 979-8-218-17300-5

Published in Atlanta, Georgia by Leadership Ministries, Inc..

Dedicated to:
My wife Suzanne Rebecca White
November 16, 1941 - October 17, 2020

Foreword

I met Chris White at a business lunch nearly ten years ago. We exchanged phone numbers. A couple of weeks later we met for lunch. Then coffee. Then a breakfast. And so it went. Chris followed up regularly. At one point he said, "If you're inclined, you ought to join us at the table on Friday mornings"—intended as a light touch but not much of a disguise. He was insistent. Eventually I showed up.

Before describing my own experience with the Friday Morning Men's Fellowship (FMMF), some context is important. After rejecting "religion" as a kid, I had lived an entirely secular adulthood. I was agnostic at best. An atheist wannabe. I had respect for credible believers as well as some of the vocal anti-theists to the extent those opposing figures developed and defended deep convictions that I couldn't muster.

At nearly fifty years of age, I heard someone say, "Fear of God is the beginning of wisdom." That gave me pause. I had always been interested in sources of wisdom. But after two graduate degrees, extensive business experience, travel to all reaches of the planet, and devouring what I understood to be great books and ideas, I had never heard a reference to wisdom put that way.

What was the source of "wisdom"? Had I not already surpassed the threshold of "beginning"? "Fear"? Yes, an effective tool maybe, but how can that be productive? And what is meant by "God"? Surely, it's a metaphor. I discovered the quote was rooted in Psalm 111 and was peppered throughout other places in the Bible. "The Bible?" I thought. "Come on." And then, "What else of value might there be in that dusty tome?" Those questions sent me on a quest to learn something of Scripture. I got a Bible. I enrolled in an intensive two-year course to study the Old and New Testaments.

Throughout my life I had been quick to debate others about the Bible. But for the first time (remarkably), it occurred to me that I had never actually read the Bible. I would never dream of perpetrating that kind of fraud in a debate about King Lear or Slaughterhouse Five or a Supreme Court case. So I started to take it seriously—as an intellectual exercise.

By the time I met Chris White I was a couple of years into this quest. At his invitation I showed up one Friday morning at an On the Border restaurant in Buckhead, like so many men before and after me. I was introduced to a roomful of guys, had a coffee and a doughnut, listened to one of the guys give a tight twenty-minute testimony, and then took a seat at Chris's table. There I found a mix of men, mostly

Elizabeth and Jody Newman

business guys in ties. Some in boots and jeans. Some young professionals, some elderly. Bankers, farmers, real estate developers, construction managers, entrepreneurs, photographers, lawyers. Guys like me.

Since that day it's been a priority and a privilege to sit with these men at the On the Border restaurant each Friday morning. What an incredible institution the FMMF has become. What a profound impact these men have had on my life. I am one of thousands marked by the FMMF over the last thirty-plus years—men who gathered at 7:00 a.m. every Friday of every week of every year to think, explore, listen, raise insights, learn, and find ways to integrate new wisdom into daily life, to be better citizens, better leaders, better fathers, better husbands.

Another week, another bit of wisdom.

Each man on his own path of transformation.

Each of us getting closer to the light.

— *Jody Daniel Newman*
Atlanta businessman

Prologue

A boy and a girl grow up on opposite sides of Southington Mountain, only about nine miles from each other, but worlds apart in other ways. The boy lives in Waterbury, Connecticut, a blue-collar factory town, and he must cope with the needs of a large family and disorder caused by little money and general discontent. The girl lives in the beautiful town of Cheshire, on the other side of the mountain. She enjoys a happy life with a harmonious, stable family of modest means. The boy and the girl meet, and God takes them places they never dreamt possible.

———————

"When Jesus said this…
the people were delighted with
all the wonderful things He
was doing." LUKE 13:17

It is my hope that the
readers of this story,
especially all those who
invested in our lives along
the way, are delighted
when they read this book.

CHRIS WHITE • FALL 2022

———————

CHAPTER 1

October 1976

It was a beautiful, sunny fall afternoon with long shadows in Saint Davids, a residential community on the Philadelphia Main Line. I was standing in the kitchen of our heavily mortgaged house in which we had just invested $25,000 to renovate the kitchen and add a fourteen-foot shed roof with a greenhouse. How would we pay for all this?

I was holding a drink in an expensive Irish crystal glass. Suddenly the back door opened, and Suzanne came down the galley kitchen straight at me. In her classic, forthright style, she said, "Today, I did what you're eventually going to have to do. Today, I asked Jesus Christ to come into my life."

The ice cubes shook in my glass. That was forty-five years ago, but I remember it as if it were yesterday.

My wife's face wore a curious expression that might have been matched by the expression of a merchant Jesus described in a parable: "Again, the kingdom of heaven is like a merchant looking for fine pearls. When he found one of great value, he went away and sold everything he had and bought it" (Matthew 13:45–46). Suzanne, too, had found it and bought it, the whole thing. No sacrifice would be too big. It was worth it.

What would become a fruitful ministry, training (especially) men in the faith, was born on that sunny afternoon in Saint Davids, Pennsylvania.

I imagine if you were to see us from the outside then, you would be impressed: the three-story Dutch Colonial under renovation, a new Ford Gran Torino station wagon, a new lime green Volkswagen "Love Bug" for Suzanne, a pair of handsome, towheaded boys—three-year-old Christopher and two-year-old Colin—and, of course, Betsy, a giant Airedale, and Thomas Jefferson, our Siamese cat. The externals were deceiving.

At this point we were in no shape to serve others. We had not been harmonizing. For the next few years, the Lord, in his grace and mercy, reordered our lives so we would become more usable in His kingdom. We were willing. We had always been best friends, but we did not have a foundation that would sustain us for the work to which He was calling us.

Training in my family of origin, and more recently in my eight years with IBM, was woefully inadequate for the job. I did not have the communication skills needed to be a full marriage partner with all the stresses on us. Especially among business colleagues in our corporate culture, they regarded expressions of emotion—"frustrated," "worried," "disappointed"—as weakness.

I had become a poster boy for the Peter Principle thesis that people in a hierarchy tend to rise to their level of incompetence. I was having a tough time adjusting to the role of marketing manager after years of being the supersalesman in New York City.

When I got home from work, I would vent angrily and not express myself effectively. Ironically, now especially, I needed good relational skills with a fantastic wife, who was having a challenging time herself. Suzanne was finding the role of mother difficult after her fast-paced career in retail fashion.

One day she hit me with, "Why do you go to work and I stay home?" She stopped me cold. I was speechless, clueless. She frightened me.

The other big issue was money. My attitude toward money was to work harder and sell my way out of debt. But those days were over. I had played that game, made and spent the money. Now, in the management business, you make money with the skill of helping other people work. And I was struggling in that job. I could not make life work! What is a man to do?

I stood out in a far corner of our property and gazed at what I saw as the potential of this fine, huge home, this monument to my ego. I was

Our house was a Dutch Colonial in Saint Davids, Pennsylvania, and we had all the trappings of success. On the outside things looked great.

starting to think there was no way I could get there from here. That was a new thought for me. There had always been a way.

A Latin expression describes what then happened: sursum corda (lift up your heart). I lifted up my heart. It was up! But I had no idea where or to whom I should lift it. Just up. My life was becoming unmanageable. I had outrun my coverage, using a football analogy, when I had married Suzanne seven years earlier, and now I was running out of options.

The afternoon that she came home with her startling revelation about finding Jesus Christ, she had been attending a women's seminar on "Marriage and Family Life God's Way," led by Pastor Bill Hogan, an evangelical Christian teaching pastor.

Fortunately, providentially, we were surrounded by a community of men and women who were authentic followers of Jesus Christ and demonstrated that reality with hospitality. A month after that episode, we found ourselves in the carriage house at the estate of Arthur and Nancy DeMoss, a prominent couple in Bryn Mawr, for a class on marriage. Pastor Bill again was teaching. It was there that I, too, met the Savior.

I will never forget those intelligent, astute, and hospitable first steps toward the cross of Jesus. Every Thursday night we met with a group of professional couples for this study. Teaching from Genesis, Pastor Bill showed that the historical account of Noah, the ark, and the flood was a foreshadowing of the new protection, the salvation given us when we accept Christ's sacrifice as an atonement for our sins. God saved Noah and his family by protecting them with the ark. Today, with His New Covenant, God saves us through the covering of Christ's shed blood.

As I listened, the Spirit of Christ, the Holy Spirit, used that scripture to overwhelm me, to shock me with grace. I slid off the folding chair and received the Lord on my knees. I was born again. I had a new heart, as John 3:3 proclaims. I will always remember "the hour I first believed."

So now, the Lord, in His will, had yoked us together in the faith. Suzanne and I were partners in the great enterprise of the Great Commission to make disciples. For the next forty-four years, until Suzanne's death in October 2020, she and I shared the adventure of following Jesus Christ together. It was an adventure like no other.

CHAPTER 2

Who Am I?

Sometime in the early 1970s I was attending IBM's 100% Club meeting at the Breakers in Palm Beach, Florida. At that time this was a gathering of mostly men who had made or beat the quota set for them by management—sort of a gathering of the stars.

We had what Ralph Waldo Emerson called "the bond of common experience." We were soldiers in suits, white shirts, and "sincere ties" (the way the IBM personnel manual prescribed dress). The way we celebrated together at such a gathering was to get perspective from top management or an inspirational speaker in the morning, recreate in the afternoon with deep sea fishing or maybe golf, and probably drink too much after dinner.

Something was missing. And that something was the gospel of forgiveness, which at this point in my life had not begun to dawn on me. There is a completely different atmosphere when a group of forgiven sinners get together. Emerson's "bond of common experience" is still there, but a whole new dimension of experience is also present.

In one of the plenary meetings, Fred Herman, an old-time motivational speaker, asked us to write down on a three-by-five card our answer to the question "Who am I?" One guy wrote, "I am a duck hunter." Another, "I am a Georgia Bulldog." Someone even wrote, "I am an IBM-er." I don't remember what I wrote down. At this time in my life, I was clueless about any kind of life's purpose. Life was a fight, and winning was always essential. If you don't win, you don't come back next year to the club. And there was nothing worse than that.

I remember, however, being terribly hung over that morning. Then Fred Herman asked for a show of hands. "How many wrote down, 'I am a child of God'?"

As I recall, no hands went up. There was a noticeable quiet in the ballroom. Fred probably planned it that way; he was an old pro. He stunned me a little. This was, after all, a business meeting of the IBM elite. At that time that meant prestige. What did God have to do with that?

What Fred Herman may have been trying to get us in touch with was our whole sense and need of identity. Who am I? How do I see myself?

How we see ourselves is fundamental to personal growth. This may be the very reason why the ministry Suzanne and I built over almost four decades seemed to click. God called us into meeting a basic human need.

When a person finds the Lord, they find their true identity as a child of God, and they are able to connect with other people with whom they share common struggles. People struggle in their marriages, their families, and their businesses. It is much harder when you have to go it alone.

When men, in particular, study the Bible together, they have a bond of common experience. But they experience something more: the supernatural presence of God. The Holy Spirit, the Spirit of Christ is there with them, and He makes all the difference. He adds another dimension. The Bible calls it fellowship. "For where two or three are gathered together in My name, there am I in the midst of them" (Matthew 18:20 KJV). This is the missing link in so many men's lives.

Men now can share common experiences: raising children, managing money, maintaining intimacy with their wives (not just sex, believe it or not), and career issues. It has been amazing to see the power of a group of men who trust each other, who trust the Lord, sharing in fellowship. The ingredients, the secret sauce for a dynamic men's fellowship, are men with common experiences in their marriages, families, and businesses. Leaders who know how to facilitate meaningful discussion about the Word of God and the Lord.

I'm not sure when I first heard the story of William Tyndale, an amazing man who saw an opportunity with the printing press in the early 1500s. Now he could get his English translation of the Bible printed by the thousands, and he was determined to make it possible for common men and women to fully explore Scripture in their own language.

Yet the clergy objected. "We are better to be without God's Law than the pope's," they said. But Tyndale replied, "If God spare my life, ere many years, I will cause a boy that driveth a plow shall know more Scripture than thou dost." He was martyred for his convictions, but Tyndale's ambition helped lead to a great reformation.

We have had the English Bible for five hundred years! Yet, I daresay for most American business and professional men, the Bible has no relevance for their God-ordained roles as leaders in their marriages, families, and businesses.

There was a time when I was one of them. When I was growing up, a big family Bible reposed under the coffee table, but to my memory no one ever read it. Yes, we did what most American families often did. We attended church, and I even went to a parochial school when I was younger.

When I was older, I refused to go through the motions any longer. After college and military service, I was just starting with IBM when I met Suzanne. To my evangelical Christian friends, I say that when I came to know Suzanne was the first time I was saved. (Sarcastic humor.) I have no doubt that God brought her into my life because He had some special work for me to do, and there was no way I would be able to do that work without her.

Several years into our marriage, the wheels started to come off our materialistic lives. After my twelve-hour day in the corporate rat race, I was drained, empty. Suzanne would meet what was left of me, ready to take out her frustrations on me. We were trapped and unhappy. Neither of us knew what else to do or where to look for answers.

The last place, the very last place, would be anything having to do with religion. But by the grace of God, in 1976, we started to meet witnessing Christians. A witnessing Christian is one who has a genuine personal relationship with the living God, Jesus Christ, and lives their life as a testimony to the reality of the risen Christ.

At the age of thirty-six, for the first time in my life, I was able to have an intelligent conversation with another man about the most important things in life: marriage, family, children, career, money. I learned Jesus is interested in all these things and gave His life to redeem us from a world that wants to run without Him. And these are the practical issues that the Bible addresses.

The decades since have been a journey, bringing me to the point of telling our story. God gave Suzanne and me three wonderful sons and meaningful work that suited us. For more than thirty years we worked together to build an organization with the potential to reach more men and their families.

The leadership role of men in American culture continues to decline under the pressures of so many major changes in our society, virtually upending not only longstanding traditions but the divine model, and creating a crisis for families. This book records the story of how we were able to help real men mature through fellowship centered on studying Scripture.

This book tells the story of the development and growth of the Friday Morning Men's Fellowship (FMMF) program and how it has reached thousands of men and changed their lives forever.

One of the longtime leaders in this dynamic program, Brian Ranck described

Brian Ranck

it this way: "Studying the Bible and the fellowship have kept me involved. Sometimes I think of the FMMF as an aircraft carrier. Stay with me. The fighter jets come back to the aircraft carrier to refuel before going back into combat. My mind and soul need this weekly landing at the FMMF to refuel. The other thing that keeps me coming back are the authentic relationships that are developed at the FMMF."

CHAPTER 3

December 25, 1940

On Christmas Day, I came into the world, the firstborn in my family. From my earliest memories, I always felt I was special to my parents, in part because I was born on the day we celebrate as the Savior's birthday and because of its significance to my Roman Catholic mother. My parents named me Christopher in honor of Saint Christopher, believed to be a third-century Christian martyr.

Receiving this name was like the blessing given by the Old Testament patriarchs to their children. It was then, is now, and always has been the attitude of approval so essential in developing children who need to get this message from their parents: "I love you just the way you are." "You are special." I had that from the day I was born. Words help. So does touch. But it all starts with an attitude of approval.

My family was Irish Catholic. Our American roots go back to 1900 when Augustine Capizuto arrived from Italy. His daughter Raphaella married Irishman Ed McCarthy in the 1920s. Their wedding was such a phenomenon that the whole town of Waterbury turned out to see it. The Irish and Italians didn't usually intermarry. It is an indelible memory imparted to me by my family in my early life. My suspicion is that the Irish side of the match got their way, and Raphaella's name was changed to Charity.

My mother, Irene, was one of the McCarthys' four daughters, who grew up in a chaotic household. My grandfather was a railroad worker, a man with an outgoing personality, and an alcoholic. Although he had no formal education, at one time he had been in vaudeville in New York, and he liked to run with powerful people, many of whom he met by attending Alcoholics Anonymous meetings. My memory is that he found peace in later life.

My mother married Marvin White. He was from a New England farming class known as Swamp Yankees, a term sometimes used in derision. They were poor farmers who received the leftovers of the land after the bankers, shipbuilders, whalers, traders, and educators settled on the coast. Moving inland, the farmers took the best land. What was left over went to the Swamp Yankees. They were not among the religious and ambitious Pilgrims who had sailed to America on the Mayflower, but rather they were more often in the ranks of the undesirables who left England after some form of misconduct. In their new land there were times when some of them lived in the swamps, giving rise to the nickname.

They lived in the woods in Colonial and Cape Cod houses built with wide boards and roughhewn rafters. Frugal by nature and necessity, they were stubborn settlers of good standing in the rural communities, but they

Left: My father Marvin White and holding me is my mother, Irene; Right: My cousin Patrick Quilter and me after church one Sunday.

Left to right, standing: My father Marvin White, mother Irene White (wearing a Thai sild dress from material I sent her from a duty-free port during my Navy days), Suzanne, Roy Schmaling (the groom), myself; seated: sister Mary Beth Schmaling and my grandmother, Charity McCarthy.

usually had only minimal formal education and little desire to augment it. And they were insular. They had little interest in venturing beyond their swamp enclaves, let alone move up. Their attitude was "We're fine. Leave us alone." They did not worry much about what was going on around them, but rather they plowed ahead to what was in front of them.

My father had to drop out of school in the eighth grade when his father died. It happened suddenly. His widowed mother and a priest showed up at his school and called him out of the classroom. He never went back to school. Young Marvin had to work to help support the family. His mother was a matron at the YMCA, making beds and cleaning rooms. He worked in a butcher shop and later a factory, and then settled into his lifetime work of driving a bus.

Affable and good-natured, he went to work very early every morning to take his bus "out of the barn," as he put it. When I was a child, there were times I would get downtown somehow and ask the bus dispatcher in the town square what route my father was driving that night. Then I rode one or two round trips with my dad and turned the handle on the fare box that counted the money. I often wore his extra bus driver's hat.

Dad was reliable and dependable, but he did not have ambitions beyond his job, not only because of his nature but also because of his circumstances. When you are pulled out of school in the eighth grade, you have little chance to meet a teacher who will take a personal interest in you and encourage you. In later years I realized my father did not have any men in his life to encourage him to strive for a developmental mind-set that would allow him to develop his full potential. Even now I think about what he might have become if he had been given some of the advantages I have had. Many people invested in me along the way, leading to my life's work in leadership development.

At home my dad smoked Chesterfield cigarettes, drank beer, and listened to baseball games on the radio. When he spoke of his background to the family, he said he was a Swamp Yankee, though he was somewhat defensive since my mother was appalled by the term and its meaning.

Mother had been an executive secretary before their marriage, and she was the disciplinarian in the family. She had little patience with such things. Four more children had come along after me, and she was keeping the household together and preparing Italian meals, including hard salami and strong provolone cheese. Meanwhile, she was trying to earn money in a variety of jobs. I remember when she worked in a factory not too far from our school. My sister and I would run down there after school and wait for the factory whistle to blow. There, in the crowd of workers, would be our exhausted mother, happy to see us. She did everything she could to make our lives better. But there was never enough money. Thinking back, I realize how much strain we were under, especially my mother.

When my father had been quite young, he visited an uncle on his farm in summertime. His uncle loved Herman Melville's Moby Dick and would read the book to Marvin, who years later often talked about it. It might have been the only good literature he knew. When I was growing up, he read only the sports section of the newspaper, but I believe he had a wistful longing to read. When he drove busloads of private school students to sporting events at rival schools, he was always impressed by how the young men would read. His uncle, by reading Moby Dick to him, had planted a seed that barely sprouted before economic necessity and poverty settled heavily on my father and his family.

———————————

Dad was reliable and dependable, but he did not have ambitions beyond his job, not only because of his nature but also because of his circumstances. In later years I realized my father did not have any men in his life to encourage him to strive for a developmental mind-set that would allow him to develop his full potential.

———————————

During those summers on the farm, his uncle also taught him how to cut hay with a scythe, honing the tool to a keen edge with a sharpening stone carried in his overall pocket. This deeply impressed my father, and he often spoke of it. How remarkable that such a simple thing made such a strong impression on him. But this speaks to how we live, as King Solomon wrote in Ecclesiastes, "If the ax is dull and its edge unsharpened, more strength is needed, but skill will bring success" (10:10). This wisdom, applied to the skill of living, gives us a great object lesson on how we can invest in our generation and posterity. By just caring enough to get involved, we can teach others what we know. The more we know, the more we can give.

CHAPTER 4

"Just Do It"

When I was growing up in Waterbury, I learned a hard work ethic and was blessed with the will to work and succeed even in the midst of poverty. When I was born, our family lived on Albion Street on the top floor of a three-story apartment house. Something I have never forgotten is the smell of stale beer and cigarette smoke emanating from the tavern on the first floor.

As I grew up, we moved to other places, one of which was no more than a shack on Division Street, where a coal-fired stove in the basement provided all the heat. If my father worked the night shift, I had to go down to the cellar in the middle of the night to tend the stove, and that was a scary thing to do for a boy of twelve. The cellar had a dirt floor, and there were rats down there. I would open the stove, shake the grate, take out the clinkers, and put in two shovels of coal. This was good training in doing the things in life that have to be done.

The neighborhood was predominantly Italian, good people. We were the only Anglo-Saxons. People tried to help each other. Nobody knew they were poor. Weddings were held in the upstairs room of the local saloon, featuring homemade sandwiches on Italian rolls and accordion music. We kids all danced the polka. These were happy times.

Thanks to my mother's insistence, as well as her willingness to beg, borrow, or steal, I was enrolled at St. Thomas Grammar School along with my sister Dianne, who was two years younger. We walked at least a mile to school every day and learned from the Sisters of Charity. They were wonderful teachers. They drilled us on the basics, phonics, grammar, and arithmetic, and they instilled in me a lifelong respect for grammar. I remember fondly learning how to diagram sentences. Structure helps me. Penmanship was also important, but they blighted mine, because whenever I misbehaved, the sisters made me go home and write the word silence a thousand times. If you have to do that, it ruins your penmanship.

From Division Street, our next move was to Broadview Acres, a brand-new federally subsidized, low-income housing project with hundreds of attached homes, solidly built of bricks. The neighborhood was still under construction when we moved into 172 Knollwood Circle. The house had three bedrooms, and that made it feel like a mansion for five children. It was situated far from downtown, away from any sort of commercial establishment. Broadview Acres became home to thousands of low-income people, both black and white. It commanded a breathtaking panoramic view of the Naugatuck Valley and the Naugatuck River, but if my family ever took notice of the spectacular view, I never knew it. We were too preoccupied with holding things together and surviving.

I rode the school bus daily to Crosby High School in downtown Waterbury. A blessing came with my physics teacher there, Mr. Kenny, a man who had found his calling was to teach. Not only was he effective in getting over the basics of how the physical world operates, but there was a tone, a look of approval, in the way he received my youthful enthusiasm when I sometimes expressed my excitement too vigorously. Mr. Kenny smiled patiently and lovingly. A life lesson is that the attitude of a teacher as to whether he enjoys his work, has the necessary aptitude and cares about his students can make all the difference in the world for a young mind. It did for me.

Outside of school, I picked apples, had a paper route, worked at Grant's Department Store, and took advantage of any opportunity to make money. I took my pay home and gave it to my mother. Some of my friends said, "Why do you give it to your mother?" But it didn't bother me. It was just a drop in the bucket, given all of our needs. My paper route had 120 customers, all in the public housing project. Delivering by hand to their doors and collecting payment was a challenge.

At Myrtle Beach in Milford, Connecticut. Uncle Pat and Aunt Mary would often share their beach house with us. My sister Dianne is here with me. She died tragically in her late 20s with her two children.

I would be on my hands and knees at Grant's, washing cabinets near the window overlooking the main street, and all the school's gladiators would come down the street with their football gear. It was not the happiest of circumstances for a teenager. But I was resilient. That's my gift. I have a lot of staying power. Swamp Yankees are noted for that. If they get in a rut, they keep plowing, and they don't care what's happening anywhere else. They just keep moving. That was a precursor to my whole life.

Recreation was a do-it-yourself challenge for me and my teenage friends. Broadview Acres was surrounded by smaller farms that people still worked, some as dairy farmers. We terrorized them. We were like an alien army camped around their farms. But we had to make our own activities for ourselves. None of us played organized sports. We would build things in the nearby woods. We chopped down trees and chased cows, herding them up. Those poor farmers. They probably had day jobs. When they came home, they would try to milk those lathered-up cows. Such futility! There were pear and apple trees on the farms, and we would strip

27

them of their fruit. We had no structured activities or outlets for our energy, so we created our own mischief.

Some of us formed a little gang, and we had a football team. But there was only one piece of equipment for the whole team: a battered red helmet contributed by Jim Spahn, an African American kid whose father had worn it when he played football in high school. We took it to our games against other teams in the adjacent communities, usually about a mile away. We couldn't use the old red helmet, as it had no chin strap. So we carried it as if it were our pennant.

As teenagers we organized ourselves according to where we lived in the community, either the northside or the southside. My team was on the northside, the high ground. We were a loose group, not a gang. Nevertheless, we stuck together, sort of the blind leading the blind. When it wasn't too hot, we played basketball in an abandoned barn on our side of Broadview Acres.

One afternoon the southside guys came to play with us. I rushed home from school that day, changed my clothes, grabbed some Fig Newtons my mother had bought at the A&P, and headed for the barn with my buddies. As I approached, a kid named Red Murphy and his Italian southside buddies were leaving. Without any warning or instigation, Red coldcocked me with a vicious right fist.

I reeled, fell to the ground, and spat out the Fig Newtons. I sprang up from the ground and went into a rage. I just started swinging. In no time at all, Red capitulated.

There was only one problem with this victory. I now had a reputation as the guy who beat Red Murphy. That was a dangerous distinction. On the southside, there were several guys who were meaner and tougher than Red. I did not want them to challenge me for the title.

But as I recall, all went well. There were no further problems.

My first high school experience at the age of thirteen was traumatic. I was thrown in with a group of boys from a very different demographic, a lot of higher-income kids. It was one big embarrassment! I did not have the clothes the other students had. I wore the same clothes every day, ironing my pants every night after coming home from school. I could not play football. That year of my life is filled with painful memories.

Out of the blue, this suddenly and dramatically changed. In 1955, two back-to-back hurricanes struck Connecticut and a major dam burst,

———————————

People tried to help
each other. Nobody knew
they were poor. Weddings
were held in the upstairs
room of the local saloon,
featuring homemade
sandwiches on Italian rolls
and accordion music.
We kids all danced the polka.
These were happy times.

———————————

causing catastrophic flooding that devastated the Naugatuck Valley and destroyed virtually everything, including the railroad. Out of this tragedy, however, came opportunities for workers to relocate the railroad away from the edge of the river. I got a railroad job with good pay to help out at home.

About the time I was going to apply for college, my grandfather McCarthy, the railroad worker, fell to his death from a trestle one night. The railroad paid my grandmother a modest settlement, which she shared with her daughters. From Mother's share, she realized her dream of owning a house. Time after time she had applied for a bank mortgage, but they kept telling her, "You just can't afford a house."

In 1958, with a $2,000 down payment, my parents bought an unfinished house for $18,000. They could not afford to pay for all the work needed to finish the structure, and so I went out there after school and worked on the house. I had to learn some skills.

One day the contractor came by when I was on my hands and knees and laying tile. He said, "What're you doing here?

"My mother sent me out here." What I did not tell him was that my Swamp Yankee DNA was telling me, "Just do it!"

I remember one thing my father said to me during this time: "Son, I don't know how you do it. You work hard and you bring the money home to your mother. You have nothing to show for it." That empathetic encouragement covered a multitude of sins.

CHAPTER 5

Suzanne

Suzanne Cuthbert was born on November 16, 1941, in Abingdon Township, Pennsylvania, just three weeks before the Japanese bombed Pearl Harbor and dragged America into the Second World War.

Her father, Harold Cuthbert, a native of England, had emigrated to Canada before moving to Pennsylvania as a salesman for the Lehigh Coal Company. Golfing was in his genes. His father, David Cuthbert, had been a pro at St. Andrews. Harold had an attractive personality, and he was the amateur golf champion of Philadelphia. He knew golf and he knew the greats, people like Jack Kelly, Grace's brother. Although Harold and his wife were of modest means, they ran in higher-class business and golf social circles. When Harold was winning amateur events, the trophies were of sterling silver

Harold and Adeleen Cuthbert

31

and were passed down in the family. And some of these treasures now grace our home.

Suzanne's mother, Adeleen, was an artist. "My parents were a very darling, handsome couple," my wife recalled. She remembered them going out on Saturday nights to the Manufacturer's Country Club all dressed up.

When Suzanne was ten, her family moved to Cheshire, Connecticut, and when she was in high school, her classmates voted her "Best Dressed"—perhaps foreshadowing her future career. She also was captain of the cheerleaders for both the football and basketball teams. Yet despite her athleticism, she had none of the Cuthbert golfing genes. "I never lifted a golf club," she said. Her younger brother, Scott, was a low-handicap golfer, however.

Childhood photo of Suzanne and brother Scott.

Suzanne's parents were supportive and caring; they always put their children's needs above their own. Later in life, this same attitude was reflected in how Suzanne raised our three sons and how she supported me.

There was no doubt in her mind about what career she would pursue: fashion and retailing. She studied retailing at Green Mountain College, a small liberal arts school near Dartmouth, where there was a good variety of gentlemen to date but not marry. Career came first. After college, she worked in nearby New Haven for six months and then moved to San Francisco with a friend, pursuing retailing and fashion.

She learned about fashion from the bottom up, working for a small fashion house. Then Suzanne became manager of the toy department for Christmas at the City of Paris, a big store in downtown San Francisco. Later she went on to head another department. After two years in San Francisco, being "very risk-oriented," as she described it, she returned to the East Coast, living in New York's Greenwich Village, working at the World's Fair,

■━━━━━━━━━━━━■

When Suzanne was ten,
her family moved to Cheshire,
Connecticut, and when
she was in high school,
her classmates voted her
"Best Dressed"—perhaps
foreshadowing her future career.
Suzanne's parents were
supportive and caring;
they always put their children's
needs above their own.

■━━━━━━━━━━━━■

to the New York Times. The Bonwit Teller building, designed in 1929, featured an entranceway "that was a stupendously luxurious mix of limestone, bronze, platinum and hammered aluminum."

Suzanne had found success and fulfillment in her chosen work, but she could not know she was being prepared for something entirely different and could not imagine what heaven had in store for her.

CHAPTER 6

"You're Going to Go Far"

My family got our first television set when I was about thirteen years old. The show *Industry on Parade* depicted various aspects of American industries, and all of that fascinated me. One of the episodes featured a sales representative for a sophisticated business. "That's me!" I decided.

That kind of job spelled success for me. No one in my family had any success in a business or profession. An uncle who studied for the priesthood had to drop out because of economics. He became a lifer at the post office. He was a stable force in the family. Education makes a big difference.

The idea of becoming an industrial salesman turned into a fixed goal for me. To reach that lofty height meant I needed a college education, which would be a first for my extended family. I enrolled in the Waterbury branch of the University of Connecticut, and without the benefit of any career counseling, I naively enrolled in the School of Engineering, pursuing my idea of being an industrial salesman. You don't need to be an engineer necessarily for such a career path, but you do need to know a lot about people. (Ironically, I would later become proficient in life and career planning, which is one of the key processes we developed and now use at the Leadership Development Company.)

During my first two years of college, I managed to pass differential calculus and wade into integral calculus, but I struggled badly. My math professor, Mrs. Phelan, told me, "I don't think this is going to work for you,

Chris. I don't think it's the right thing for you." She was right. I am not an engineer. My professor was trying to help me. It was a small town and this was a small branch of the University of Connecticut with local people who cared. I flunked out.

The process required me to go before a faculty committee before I was drummed out. There were several faculty members in the meeting, including Mrs. Phelan and an older English professor. He asked me, "How did you end up in the School of Engineering?"

I said, "In high school, I took the Kuder preference test that asked, would you rather be a garbage man or an engineer? I put down engineer, but today, to tell you the truth, Professor, I'd rather be a garbage man."

He laughed and said, "Mr. White, you're going to go far."

There it was again. The tone, the look, the words of approval and encouragement. I took these experiences to heart. I would need them. Thank God for men like that professor, leaders who care!

It was the kind of positive reinforcement I valued. I remembered anything anybody said to me that was positive and encouraging. In high school, after I answered a question or gave a word in English class, Mr. McCarthy said, "Mr. White, you have one of the best vocabularies in this class." Words and language are important to me. In the culture we built at the Leadership companies, the number-one correlation in the things we measure in business success and life success is vocabulary. Imagine not learning that until you are in your forties.

I learned there are various people along our way who give an encouraging word and show some personal interest, and it makes all the difference in the world. Studies bear that out. Personal interest in a person: that is where you start. It is the first step in any professional capacity.

After I flunked out of college, I could not re-enroll for six months, so I went back to working on the railroad. Since it was summertime, I was around several young men who were my age. So we had a crew of college-aged men mixed in with chronic alcoholics who had seen better days. Everything on the railroad is heavy. The crushed stone ballast under the ties is heavy. The ties are heavy. And the rails are really heavy. But I was strong, and I brought home seventy-five dollars a week, which was a godsend to my mother.

I will never forget two characters from that railroad experience. One was Mundo, an older Italian immigrant who sat in the front corner, out of the way in the covered truck that took us to the job site. He carried a big lunch pail packed carefully with Italian cheese and salami sandwiches and homemade wine. Some of the guys who were hungover distanced themselves from him and his rich odors. I was raised to appreciate those smells, however.

Right there among the foolish college guys and the grizzled alcoholics, Mundo was an island of quiet contentment. He stood out. I envied him in a way. I found out he and his wife had their own small house, where he grew grapes, raised chickens, and tended a small garden.

During the day he worked quietly, paced himself, and kept himself totally dressed in a long-sleeved shirt and a big hat. He did not let the sun beat him down. As Christ said, "Peace I leave with you; my peace I give you. I do not give to you as the world gives" (John 14:27). I admired his peacefulness, but I would not have that myself for another sixteen years.

John Glenn was the big boss. His black railroad Chevy sedan with black tires and a spotlight on the driver's side would drive up to the job site once a day. John would march down the tracks toward us, with two assistants, looking like he was spoiling for a fight. He ignored the foremen and started yelling as soon as he saw us.

One day we were inside a big hopper car, making sure the ballast kept moving down the slide. It was terribly hot in there. John, with his high-buckled black shoes, stood at the top of the ladder on the outside of the hopper car and screamed, "Come on, you laggards, what do you think this is, a Sunday school picnic?" That was a curious analogy to me, because I had never been to a Sunday school picnic. He acted like the louder he screamed, the harder we would work. He was right. Fortunately, he had other projects to oversee.

Mundo and John Glenn were starkly contrasting figures. John saw himself as important and powerful. Mundo was a man of humility. Something inside me told me that Mundo was the better man, the one to emulate. That summer railroad job was a memorable experience.

I worked for the railroad for six months, and then I went back to the University of Connecticut and switched to a liberal arts program, which was as far from industrial engineering as I could get. I started studying what I enjoyed: history, English, political science, and sociology.

The anthropology professor started off his class by making sure we all bought into his strong bias toward macro-Darwinian evolution, essen-

———————

I learned there are
various people along our
way who give an encouraging
word and show some personal
interest, and it makes all the
difference in the world.
Studies bear that out.
Personal interest in a person:
that is where you start.
It is the first step in any
professional capacity.

———————

tially that all life on the planet evolved by a process of random selection from lower forms of life, plants, and animals. For example, human beings, homo sapiens, evolved from apes, without an outside "intelligent designer." The key to passing the course was to parrot all of his arguments for that theory back to him. And they were compelling.

One day he was feeling particularly bold and angry, and he went right at it. "You have all been brought up to believe that God did all of this," he declared. "There is no God!"

He was adamant. None of us had any real training in our Christian faith, and so no one had the courage to respond. Not a peep. I still remember that professor in his white shirt, now grayish yellow with age, and long in the tooth, wagging his finger and polemicizing, "There is no God!" It made a big impression on me. But I, too, was a biblical ignoramus—although not forever, gratefully.

After completing the first two years of higher education in my hometown, I enrolled at the main campus in Storrs—just a little less than sixty miles away. But Storrs was a completely different social climate from Waterbury. I was recruited by one of the "better" fraternities, which meant they got drunk more and had more jocks than the other fraternities. There were fifty-something guys in my fraternity, many of them from upper-income Fairfield County. Their parents were business executives who commuted to New York.

While many of the guys received checks from home for spending money, I got a job washing dishes at a Jewish sorority at night. They were lovely women, and they helped me by typing my papers. I made a little money in an attempt to compete socially. The sorority paid me ten dollars a week plus my dinner.

My roommate was a sharp, handsome Jewish guy, Dick Galley. He said, "I'm the token Jew." He enjoyed that distinction and became a good friend, which meant a lot to me. A subtopic and important part of my life has been a connection with Jewish people, including having a Jewish girlfriend in high school. The evolution of my thinking and my training has brought me to understand how remarkable God's chosen people are and what a tragedy it is that many of them, as well as Gentiles, really do not understand their true spiritual heritage. It also saddens me that there is still so much ignorance and prejudice against Jews.

Now, breaking into a new socioeconomic group at the main campus had its hazards. I was so proud of my father when he and my mother came for parents' weekend at the fraternity. He was a handsome man and wore a new suit. When an advertising executive from New York asked him what business he was in, my father simply said, "The transportation business."

But some of the fraternity guys had a lot of fun at my expense after one of them saw a letter addressed to Christopher Marvin White. For the next two years, I was the brunt of jokes with "Marvin" as the punch line. They would always embarrass me at a party. Young men like that, when they're thrown together, can be horribly cruel. But I got through it. The Swamp Yankee survived. This was another way that God, in His sovereignty, would prepare me to "stand alone."

CHAPTER 7

Anchors Aweigh

I took five years to graduate from the University of Connecticut because of the interruption when I'd flunked out, but in June 1963, I had a double major in history and political science, which was a good combination to start building a broad-base education. Later in life I would come to understand how important that is.

Always delving into the etymology of words, I asked a professor about the meaning of politics in a political science class. He looked at me as if to say, "That's what we ought to be talking about here." But the question was not on the finals. My inquiry stemmed from my nearly lifelong interest in words, which is not only extremely relevant to success in life but also an integral component of our leadership work today.

Although I did not do as well in college as I would have liked, and I lacked direction, still a door of opportunity unexpectedly opened for me. I came out of the university at the time of the roaring military-industrial complex on the front side of Vietnam. I did not know what I wanted to do right after college, but I soon found an answer.

A navy recruiter was on the campus, a young lieutenant, and he asked me to get him a date with a girl I knew. I hung out with the lieutenant for a day and took in his recruiting pitch, leading me to apply to Naval Officers Candidate School in Newport, Rhode Island. I was accepted and entered the program in the fall of 1963.

To say the navy was hungry for bodies at the time would be an understatement. With the Vietnam War imminent, there was a need for a lot of "black shoes"—young officers to do the work. It was no surprise I wound up in communication, which involved handling and editing teletype messages. The navy's assessment of my qualifications was expressed after I took the required tests: "He's about words." Later, as a result, I was given a small office on a ship to proofread teletypes, the navy's chief means of communication.

For the first time in my life, I was thrown in with men from all over the country, and my ability to cope was tested. The officer candidate in charge of our company was Robert E. Lee Green, whose name bespoke his Southern heritage as did his drawl. I figured he got the leadership job because he had been in the Reserve Officers' Training Corps (ROTC). He took his job

In the Navy I graduated OCS as an Ensign and served aboard the Carrier USS Boxer.

very seriously, which offered a challenge for me at a stage in my life when I was rebellious. With company commander Green, I started rebelling right away. He was like the rest of us, but he was in charge. So I gravitated toward the wise guys in our company. We were extending our childhood.

Green picked up that I was a wise guy. He was going to straighten me out. He assigned me to scrub out a garbage can, or GI can, in the middle of the barracks. It was a nasty job that was done by hand, but I thought there had to be a better way to carry out Green's order without doing all the dirty work he envisioned for me. I went on a sort of reconnaissance tour of the chow hall and saw that the sailors in charge of the scullery were using a steam jenny to clean out GI cans from the galley.

I enlisted a buddy, Gerald Kirschenbaum from New York, to help with my plan to clean the barracks GI can. He and I hauled the can to the chow hall. We cleaned it out almost effortlessly and very efficiently with the steam jenny.

When Green saw me later, he immediately pounced. "Mr. White, I told you to clean the GI can."

I replied, "What makes you think I didn't?" I showed him the clean can. His face showed surprise. That incident proved to me that whatever the challenge, I was determined to meet it. That is how I am. I do not know how, but I will make it work. I will get it done.

When I graduated from OCS in 1964, my parents proudly attended the ceremony. I now had the rank of ensign in the navy, a spanking new blue dress uniform, and a government check. Things were coming together beautifully for me.

I drove from my hometown in a seventy-five-dollar car—an old French Simca Aronde, a reliable runner—to report to my first duty station aboard the USS Boxer, an Essex-class aircraft carrier, which was in dry dock and being refitted at the navy yard in Portsmouth, Virginia. When I reported for duty, there was a cloud of acetylene fumes from all the welding throughout the passageways. The Boxer, commissioned in 1945 and actively deployed in the Pacific, had provided air support for United Nations forces during the Korean War and also took part in the 1962 Cuban missile crisis. The ship was deployed to Vietnam from 1965 to 1966 before being decommissioned in 1969.

Boarding the Boxer, I went up the gangplank in my spotless, immaculate Brooks Brothers uniform and smartly saluted the flag. "Ensign White reporting for duty, sir!" Naively, I thought one of the crew would help me carry my bags aboard. Lieutenant Tony, the officer of the deck, laughed cynically. I carried my own bags. My first reality check as a naval officer.

But I had the good fortune to be assigned to a stateroom with Virgil Macaluso, an Italian American from Upstate New York, the ship's lawyer. He became my Fonz. He read James Bond novels and sported a Rolex watch. Later, I lived in an apartment off the ship and, at Virgil's suggestion, bought a Gerard stereo with four records, part of his effort to educate me in the ways of the world. This was my first-ever purchase of anything electronic. Virgil, my mentor and lasting friend, later was in my wedding.

I went up the gangplank
in my spotless, immaculate Brooks
Brothers uniform
and smartly saluted the flag.
"Ensign White reporting
for duty, sir!" Naively,
I thought one of the crew
would help me carry my bags
aboard. Lieutenant Tony,
the officer of the deck,
laughed cynically.
I carried my own bags.

I served aboard the Boxer for two years, then transferred to Norfolk, on a NATO Staff.

I was part of a team of five officers who reported to Lt. Cdr. Benny Goodman, the chief information officer from the U.S. Naval Academy and a good, kind man. We were now in the amphibious "Gator Navy," the term for ships used to transport Marine Corps landing forces and supplies to beaches.

The Boxer was deployed for exercises in the Caribbean, opening multiple opportunities for problems for me. Boredom was my enemy at this time because of my choleric temperament, and there was little to do, especially during the long voyages, tempting me to drink and get into trouble in liberty ports like Charlotte Amalie in the Virgin Islands. This was easy to do because the navy was what I would call an alcoholic culture. There was plenty to drink "on the beach" all the time, and on a cruise to the Caribbean, I drank too much and got into too many fights. I was on a collision course with much bigger trouble and didn't know it.

My friend Virgil gave me the wakeup call I needed. He said, "Chris, you're a topic of conversation in the captain's meetings with the executive staff." That got my attention like a slap in the face. Quickly, I shaped up in the nick of time to avoid the serious consequences that loomed ahead of me. It was a life lesson. It was grace!

For two years I served on the Boxer before transferring to a NATO staff job in Norfolk under Adm. Thomas H. Moorer, a World War II hero whose distinguished career included serving as chief of naval operations and chairman of the Joint Chiefs of Staff, as well as NATO supreme allied commander, Atlantic. I was promoted to lieutenant, junior grade.

I had free time on my hands when I had the evening and midwatches, so I earned a real estate license in Virginia and landed a job with a developer, George Goldberg, who was marketing some property on Hatteras Island, North Carolina, a beautiful barrier island. I worked off-hours to show properties and earned a 10 percent commission.

One day a wealthy widow drove down from Norfolk with me in my brand-new Volvo to Hatteras to look at some lots. There were two large lots on a dune, and each was priced at $10,000. "I'll take both of them," she said.

Goldberg's reaction: "I can't believe this!" He handed me a contract, and I went back to the widow's house to get her signature.

She saw Goldberg's name and asked, "Is he a Jew? My husband told me to never do business with a Jew." Alarm bells went off. Was I going to lose this deal and the $2,000 commission? I held my breath, but she signed. Then the lady said, "Now that I have the property, I want to build houses. What do I do?"

I said, "You come to me."

When I told Goldberg, he said, "Chris, you are going to go far."

I was honing my skills all this time for the Lord's future assignment. At this point, I did not have a clue about anything spiritual, anything out of this world.

CHAPTER 8

Navy Blue to Big Blue

It was time to leave the navy after four years. I was twenty-seven and did not know what to do. There was no history of success in my family. Only my uncle Pat could be so considered, and he was a lifer in the post office. Uncle Al, my father's sister's husband, was a licensed master electrician. I really liked him. He also happened to be Jewish. Everybody else in my family was blue collar, a factory worker or a bus driver, like my father.

I decided I was going to be an industrial salesman after all. With no training in this field, I took a correspondence course in diesel engines through the U.S. Armed Forces Institute. It was a good way to put some focus on the job hunt. I loved cars and engines. Still do.

I was in a good spot to find a job. The four years in the navy, on top of college, made me a good entry-level corporate prospect, and I connected with Lehman Association, a company specializing in placing men like me. Then I made a hobby of going for interviews with Fortune 500 companies, all expenses paid. I did two a month. I had plenty of chances.

At Caterpillar Tractor in Peoria, they laughed me off. But at Cummins Engine Company in Columbus, Indiana, the human resources guy loved me. He felt they needed a communicator, not a technician, in the Customer Service Department. The guy in charge of that department, however, looked at me and disagreed. "He doesn't know anything about diesel engines," he said.

The HR guy argued. "He'll learn."

But the other guy said sarcastically, "That's all I need." So there were no job offers forthcoming.

West Virginia Pulp and Paper Company on Park Avenue in New York was looking for industrial salesmen. The company psychologist, a PhD, took me to lunch with him and his secretary. I was rejected. It made me so angry I took his secretary out and persuaded her to tell me why I was turned down. "He thought you were too aggressive for this company," she said. It would not be the first time I would hear that in the years to come.

One company showed a lot of interest in me. Carrier Air Conditioning of Syracuse, New York. Of course, I knew nothing about air conditioning. But they saw something in me and hired me. One of the big reasons I took the job was the New York City location. It would give me a great vantage point from which to understand American business.

In 1967, as part of my first job out of the navy, I was sent to train with Carrier's supersalesman, Morty Specter. Not only was he a highly successful salesman, but he had a direct and wry approach, telling me when we met, "Chris, I'm the token Jew of the Carrier Air Conditioning Company." Then he assured me, "I make people heroes fast." We got off to a great start. Once again, a Jewish friend made a difference in my life.

For the next fourteen months Morty took me with him to meet with consulting architects in charge of planning and setting the specifications for the national headquarters of several retail companies. The objective was to get Carrier specified in the construction plans for those companies around the country. Morty had developed great relationships with these people to the point he could jokingly threaten bodily harm, "If those plans come out and Carrier is not specified, I will cut your — off."

This was true consultative selling, building rapport, and building equity through service. This would become my career. It started with knowing what you were talking about, followed by the consultative, empathetic stage, and finally selling—getting the order. Morty was a great mentor, a quintessential industrial salesman. I loved him.

I will never forget one call on a customer with Morty. The Jewish owner of a low-end women's clothing chain sat on his side of the desk in a large, cold warehouse full of racks of cheap dresses. Morty did his usual professional direct sales work efficiently, picking up on the man's impatient personality. The man signed, but I kept talking! This caused some tension, enough you could actually feel it. The owner glowered at me, "Do, do!" I will never forget that lesson in sales communication. Stop talking!

Finally, Mortimer told me, "You're doing a real good job." My career with Carrier was launched. For about a year I traveled all over the Northeast and trained dealers in the latest residential air-conditioning products. I was successful, resulting in wholesalers trying to hire me away from Carrier. But now I was starting to realize I was in the wrong corporate culture. The company was dominated by engineers, not sales or marketing people.

I had bought a Volvo 122S sport sedan for $2,100 (same as my commission for selling two lots of sand on Hatteras Island). It was gun-metal gray with a red Naugahyde interior. I had a rent-controlled apartment in New York City. I was in the navy reserve, attending meetings at the Brooklyn Navy Yard, and drawing $200 a month. A big bonus was that I was surrounded by cool guys. One of them, Greg Comerford, a lawyer, asked, "What do you do?"

When I said, "I'm a salesman for Carrier Air Conditioning Company," he belittled it. It was low on the career totem pole.

Greg was with International Business Machines Corporation (IBM). He said, "I want you to meet my boss." My life was about to change. This was in 1968, right on the cusp of IBM's dominating the entire computer industry.

In short order I was sitting across from an IBM executive, George Fisher, at 2 Penn Plaza in Manhattan. He blew smoke from his cigar and looked me over. "What are your strengths?"

"I'm a great salesman."

Fisher puffed the cigar. "How would you like to make $20,000 a year?"

State-of-the-art IBM computer, circa 1967.

I did not think twice. It was double my salary at Carrier. (Later, I would find it even better, as I actually made $30,000 my first year due to beating my quota.) I quit my job with Carrier and went to work for IBM in a new division, which turned out to be a great advantage for me because it played to my strength as a developer.

I had to go through computer training at the IBM school in Newark, New Jersey, which proved terribly uncomfortable. I did not have the aptitude for the technology, and they trained salesmen and systems engineers in the same course. There were days when I did not understand a word I heard.

When the technology training was over, I was with about twenty guys in a sales bullpen at 2 Penn Plaza. Everybody had a phone and a file cabinet. Not even a copy machine. Not even a touch-tone phone. That was it. I sat between a guy from Harvard and a guy from Wharton, who were a little ahead of me in seniority, and I became their slave. They trained me.

One guy had all the phone numbers lined up ready to go every day with calls to prospects. He was a model of time management. I was now into something I enjoyed and a proud salesman for IBM. Within six to eight months, the Harvard and Wharton guys were both gone, and I was still there because I am a salesman. I was smart, I was good, and I was ambitious.

I started with IBM on June 1, 1968, and would spend the next ten years with Big Blue. The first five years were great. Now I had a story to tell at the cocktail parties. IBM was prestigious, and the commissions were tremendous. I had arrived! For several years my time with IBM was very prosperous. I had found a spot where I shone as a kind of supersalesman. And then management asked me to help with marketing projects and training new salesmen.

Much bigger and better things were in store, coming in unexpected ways, starting with a call to an old Boxer shipmate, John Platte, in the summer of 1968. He had been in New York for about a year. "You need to come out to the beach house in the Hamptons," he said.

CHAPTER 9

Point of No Return

The Hamptons on the east end of Long Island offered one of the country's most attractive seaside resorts with popular summer colonies. Young singles from New York bought rent shares in the old houses for the summer. These were the big arks built behind the dunes on the Atlantic Ocean by the Wall Street fat cats in the early twentieth century.

After the call from my old shipmate, I jumped into my brand-new Volvo, stopped at a department store, and bought shorts and a shirt. Now I was ready for whatever awaited me. I drove to the Hamptons and joined with some more established guys in putting money in a pot at a party for a lobster dinner. I donated my last twenty dollars. I was flat broke.

Suzanne Cuthbert was spending her weekends in East Hampton during that summer of 1968, as she was a shareholder in one of the houses. She could afford the cost with her salary as the ladies' sportswear buyer for Bonwit Teller.

I met her for the first time at that lobster dinner. She was a knockout blonde, and she was there without her boyfriend, as he was in Germany at the time.

Saturday night she had a bottle of Beefeater gin. I said, "If you share your bottle, I'll be your date." After that party we went out and crashed other parties. She seemed to like something daring. Two entrepreneurs.

The next day I took her for a drive. She had to go by the post office and mail a letter to her boyfriend, Miles. That was the last ever mention of Miles!

From that moment we did everything together. I took her to a French restaurant where I had studied the menu earlier and snowed this gutsy girl with my French. I had never met a woman like her. She had the attitude, as I came to understand later, of "make your husband a success." I got a hint of this when we went to an architectural party, and she came back with a dinner plate from the buffet and said, "I made this for you." Here was a woman who loved to serve.

I had never experienced anything like it, a terrific woman in every way. In the fall of 1968, I had gradually come to the point of no return.

One day I said, "Let's go up to my apartment and talk." I had a thought that had not come to me until then. "We've been hanging out for a while. We like the same things," I said. "Why don't we get married?" That was the proposal. I will never forget the look on her face as she considered this, but not for too long.

She said, "Okay. I'll take care of everything. I don't like diamond engagement rings." (As I recall from more than fifty years ago, elephant-hair rings were "in" with her fashion colleagues.) "I'll buy the ring and take care of the wedding plans," Suzanne said.

She was a nonconformist, and she remained that way for the next fifty-two years. I always hoped I would leave this world before Suzanne, because once I had her in my life, I could not envision life without her. But God had other plans. I am thankful that she is with the Lord.

We were married in April 1969. I was twenty-eight; she was twenty-seven. Friday night my family hosted a dinner for the wedding party at our house. It was nothing fancy. Suzanne was gracious and included my three sisters in the wedding party. We had a modest wedding reception.

The priest gave us his counsel, but we were not very receptive. Nevertheless, he said something prophetic to these two materialistic people: "You are going to need the Lord."

We moved into my apartment in New York. I got a credit card from the Chemical Bank in New York, a gold card with the sky as the limit. We honeymooned at the Buccaneer on St. Croix. I was drinking rum in the morning—"Cruzan mornings." We were two vagabonds from Connecticut in the tropics.

Back home again, I was starting to make a little money. The first thing Suzanne did was to march me into Brooks Brothers and buy three suits. We spent $1,000 in one trip. "You're married to me. You're going to look good," she said.

She later acknowledged, "I thought Chris was going to be president of IBM. He was ambitious and strong. That attracted me because I'm rather strong. I needed somebody like him."

Those early years in Manhattan with Suzanne were fun, and they are fine memories to this day. We were best friends. We enjoyed one another without much weight on either of us at that point in our lives. There would be plenty of time for that. In the summer we would enjoy Jones Beach, about an hour east on Long Island. Determined not to sit in traffic, we would get up early Sunday morning, stop in Queens for some White Tower breakfast to go, and enjoy sitting on the beautiful beach with our two small folding chairs while having breakfast. We would leave the beach by early afternoon and see all the cars coming toward us on the Long Island Expressway. They were bumper to bumper. We were pretty satisfied with our self-centered selves. Beating the system!

That first winter, close to Christmas, I was in a prosperous mood, and one day I decided to walk home from the office rather than take the subway. I went by Bloomingdale's in midtown and bought Suzanne an A-line mink coat and a pair of leather pants to go with the coat. Was she stunning in that outfit! Spending money is fun.

Suzanne had friends in Bedford Village, about an hour north of the city, Jeff and Wendy Tweedy. And they were tweedy! Jeff was a Wall Street lawyer, and Wendy was a very with-it, pretty brunette. They had bought a fixer-upper with a lot of property. I pounded a few nails with Jeff on a couple of weekend visits. Some dormant juices started to flow.

Our first house was in Bedford Village, New York. The center of the house, a farmer's house, was built in 1793.

53

One weekend while we were riding around with Jeff and Wendy on Middle Patent Road in Bedford Village, I saw a small house for sale on four acres with a pond. The original house was built in 1793, and I bought it without thinking about it, paying $47,500. At this time in our lives, Suzanne was willing to go along with my impulsive schemes. We moved to the country and commuted together to New York.

For three years the routine was the same. Go to work, make money, invite friends up, drink French wine on a Saturday night, enjoy a fire in the fireplace. I became a bit of an antiquarian and restored the oldest part of the house. When Suzanne was eight months' pregnant, I had her glazing windows. Years later she told me she started to hate that house because all I did was work on it every weekend.

This period of our lives was all ego for me. I had no real training, and I had never been exposed to good marriage models. This would not sustain us. Before too long, the shocks necessary to get my attention started to come.

CHAPTER 10

Searching for Answers

After five years as a salesman in New York, I was promoted to a position working for the eastern regional manager and traveling the eastern United States as a resource to local management. This career move was designed to give me some strategic exposure and perspective on the business.

During this time I had a chance to work with two consultants who were hired to develop a marketing campaign for our new stable (family) of mini-management information systems (MINI MIS). I will avoid false bashfulness here and admit that I was a key to our success.

We developed a campaign called the Forgotten Manager. We gave the field sales force a message: "Mr. Corporate Manager, who isn't being served by the IT bureaucracy in your corporation, we're here to help you solve your problem. You are forgotten no more." The campaign was a smash! At least for a while. I was still in my sweet spot with creative strategic marketing and sales.

In the early 1970s I was thirty-three, and after that year at headquarters, IBM hesitated but took a chance and put me in the field as a marketing manager. The Philadelphia office was in trouble. I was assigned there with a guy from Ohio, Art Oratorio, the new manager of the entire Philadelphia operation. Art was the consummate people manager, and the men Art trained went on to become CEOs of Fortune 500 companies.

My job was to clean house and hire and train better salesmen. After about six months, Art called me into his office and said, "Sit down." I sensed trouble because his lips were quivering nervously. He was not a confrontational personality. My guard was up.

"Over the last few months, twelve people have been in here to see me," he said. "They say that if you don't leave, they are all going to quit." Later he admitted to some hyperbole, but he had successfully shattered my poor ego. He hit me so hard that I wept!

We met for six hours. I knew I had to make a restart.

This was grace. It was a step the Lord used in getting my attention. I had to get off pure ego. Before that, nobody ever took me on. Now I was going from sales to management, and Art said, "People have to love you or you aren't going to be able to lead them." I had been threatening and demanding performance, which a lot of the salesmen did not have the capacity to do. My attitude was arrogant, egotistical, and me-centric.

I went home and told Suzanne. She said, "Well, you had better listen to him!"

I was especially weak when it came time to put on my political hat for the guys from headquarters. When they challenged my strategy, I became defensive, even belligerent. The basic problem for me was that I was miscast. I had drifted into this situation because I never had a plan. I am not a big company person, I don't particularly like computers, and I am entrepreneurial, enterprising. I am not a manager! Professional assessment later revealed that, as a developmental thinker, I need to be out front, helping to shape strategy, not further down the food chain in the corporate hierarchy.

Suzanne pregnant with Chrisopher and holding our dog, Betsy.

Our son Christopher was born on October 9, 1972. We had moved to St. Davids, outside Philadelphia, into a Dutch Colonial house with four bedrooms, three baths, and a playroom over the garage. As always, a fixer-upper. It was a great neighborhood with good neighbors. Our second son, Colin, was born July 31, 1974.

Staying home and raising the children was rough for Suzanne. She did not like the new role of motherhood. Worse, when I came home, I did not know how I was supposed to help. I'd put my briefcase down for a minute and take a deep breath. What is going to be the battle du jour?

We began to search for something more in our lives. Suzanne got us into transcendental meditation. We did a lot of reading on vacation in the Caribbean. Our neighbor Charlie, a dropout minister and now college professor, and his wife gave us five self-help books. They were not much help. Each said something different from the others. I got into Napoleon Hill, author of the best seller *Think and Grow Rich.* I kept trying to find something, but I wasn't sure about what I was looking for.

The last place I would have considered was anything to do with religion. I had been inoculated early in life. All the while, God the Father was drawing us. ("No one can come to Me unless the Father who sent Me draws them, and I will raise them up on the last day" John 6:44). The very first signal out of heaven came when I was in my new white Gran Torino station wagon and heading for the office. The only thing I could get on the radio that was positive was Harry Bristow, a Christian disc jockey broadcasting from Camden, New Jersey. He was happy, joyous.

Suzanne and I were socialites, always going to parties. At one of the parties, Suzanne was telling a neighbor who had moved from the South, Mary Joe, about how great transcendental meditation was. "Suzanne, have you ever tried a Bible study?" Mary Joe asked.

Suzanne had never heard of Bible study. She grew up in a family who fit the stereotype described as "Christmas-Easter Episcopalians," rarely going to church or taking part in its activities. Mary Joe brought over a tape that explained that transcendental meditation was a form of Hindu religion. We stopped meditation. We did not want to become Hindus.

At another party another woman remarked that she had been converted. "What is that?" Suzanne wondered. Her new friend shared some books about Christianity. All that summer, Suzanne read the books. She began to understand who Jesus was. She understood she was a sinner. Then she gave me the books.

We both started reading Christian apologetics, that is, logical arguments for faith. A knockout for both of us was *Mere Christianity,* the 1952 classic by C. S. Lewis. I was thunderstruck by Lewis's declaration: "Love is an affair of the will, not of the emotions." I was starting to think maybe there was more to Christianity than I had thought.

One Sunday morning, to give Suzanne a break, I made her breakfast, found a church in the phone book that had a nursery, and dressed the boys, which gave her some peace and quiet.

At the service, they read from *The Velveteen Rabbit,* a children's book about love. Then the rector gave a sermon centered on the idea of Jesus Christ's claim of deity. His tone, his attitude was derisive, contemptible. Everyone was laughing at the idea that Jesus claimed to be God. Everyone laughed but me. Instead, surrounded by laughter, I became sick to my stomach. I had stumbled upon a fake church—a place for dropout Catholics and Protestants and Jews. The sick feeling I had was God's grace!

CHAPTER 11

Finding Faith

Suzanne's Southern friend asked her to attend that well known Christian women's "Feminar" in October 1976, at the nationally renowned Malvern Retreat House, with a group of intelligent, with-it women. Suzanne went as a radical, liberated woman to find Pastor Bill Hogan with an open Bible teaching on "Marriage and Family God's Way."

"I was doing marriage Suzanne's way," she said later.

It was the first time in her life—and she was thirty-five years old—to hear someone teach from the Bible. At the conclusion of the seminar, cards were handed out, and Pastor Bill offered a prayer for inviting Jesus into the life of anyone needing him. Suzanne said the prayer and checked the card. When she came home and told me about it, I knew immediately what was up. This was bigger than both of us.

Dick Woike's wife, Patricia, called and came by to follow up with Suzanne. But Suzanne was ahead of her. As soon as Pat got out of her Chevy with her big black Bible and knocked on the door, Suzanne met her saying, "I know what I did. You don't have to explain it to me." They became friends. "How beautiful are the feet of them that preach the gospel" (Romans 10:15 KJV).

In 1976 I had been involved in a side venture with some guys to use technology in advertising and publishing. Tom Paradis, who worked in IBM's Philadelphia office, had designed a machine that would allow a client to build his own magazine around special interests. The machine would collate articles and appropriate advertising—foreshadowing the Internet by ten years. The genius was in developing a way to capture customer-buying patterns that would be invaluable. I got to know Tom, and we began to make plans to sell the machine to advertisers. Tom gave me 10 percent of the pre-incorporation stock.

A bond broker in Philadelphia, after listening to the presentation I had created, agreed to invest $25,000 in the venture. When the broker went home that night and told his wife, she told him he was crazy. He called and backed out. Years later, after I quit the venture, Tom sold the idea for $6 million. I left the enterprise when I realized I was in serious jeopardy from overload. That was more grace!

One Monday night the Woikes picked us up in their Chevy, and for the first time we ended up at a couples' Bible class. Dick took a seat in a winged armchair, with a Bible in his lap, and taught from the gospel

A visit to the home of Arthur DeMoss turned out to be a life-changing event.

of John. The tone was upbeat and enthralling.

At the other end of the living room sat an interesting-looking man who kept glancing at me. After the class ended, he came up and said, "I'm inviting you and your wife to my house on Friday night." He was Arthur DeMoss, founder and chief executive of the National Liberty Corporation, a direct marketing insurance company.

Art DeMoss was zealous in evangelism. A mathematical genius, he had applied his talents to bookmaking for horse racing earlier in his life. One day as he left the house, his Greek mother told him, "Arthur, I am praying for you." On his way to the racetrack, he was drawn to a tent meeting nearby with a banner proclaiming "Jesus Saves." The preacher was a converted Jewish lawyer, Hyman Appleman, who spoke to Art's heart with facts and logic. Art went into the tent unconverted and came out a Christian.

He later applied his mathematical talents to the insurance business. He developed methods of selling life insurance direct to the end user.

At his house, he had movie stars and celebrities talking about their faith: Art Linkletter, Roy Rogers, Dale Evans, Tom Landry, Roger Staubach, and others. And he used them as a draw, applying his marketing skills to evangelism. He had great success.

That Friday evening we showed up at the imposing DeMoss home, known as Laurier, with seven other couples. After a lovely buffet dinner, Art asked everyone to gather in a comfortable room adjacent to the dining room. We sat in a circle on soft, comfortable chairs in anticipation. He began by reading a short passage from Peter's first epistle: "Praise be to the God and Father of our Lord Jesus Christ! In his great mercy He has given us new birth into a living hope through the resurrection of Jesus Christ from the dead" (1 Peter 1:3).

Then Art called on each person to share where he or she was "on the spiritual pilgrimage." He told us, "Tonight we will be the speakers." I was watching a master evangelist at work. What superlative technique it was to ask us that question and get us involved! When our turn came, Suzanne went first, sharing how she had attended the women's Feminar and knew exactly what she had done when she prayed to receive Christ there. She was as sharp as a tack.

I was still sorting things out. It was clear I needed more time.

Three weeks later, in a Bible study at Laurier in the converted carriage house rebuilt for that purpose, I, too, met the Savior. I was born again.

Soon I was sharing my new faith. A new convert is by far the best evangelist. Joy is the propulsion. First, I received cards with the names of people who attended the DeMoss dinner parties. I called and said I was a friend of Art's. "You were at the dinner party," I said, following the tried-and-true model. "I would like to meet you and get better acquainted." About half of those I contacted accepted my invitation to lunch or breakfast. This provided neutral ground for businessmen as opposed to a church setting.

For one-on-one meetings with businesspeople in restaurants, we used an acronym: FIRE. It stood for Family ("Tell me about your family"), Interest ("What's your line of work or career?"), Religious background ("What do you believe?"), Experience of the host ("Let me tell you what happened to me"). Best practices!

My IBM background was helpful for me. It was somewhat prestigious early on, and people were impressed. I also got together for study with some men at a Howard Johnson's restaurant.

There were three steps to bringing along new people: invite them to a dinner party, communicate with them personally and individually, and then get them into a group.

My witness to God's grace in my life extended to my workplace. To each person in my office, I brought up and explained the plan of salvation. My testimony created reverberations from management: "Chris, you're imposing your values on other people."

But I was on fire. Jesus had saved me from my sins. I also shared my story with all levels of management above me, including the president's wife, whom I had the privilege of sitting next to on the tour bus on an awards trip through the Loire Valley in France. I read scripture to her from the book of Isaiah. This lovely woman said, "That is the most beautiful thing I have ever heard." I asked her if she would like to have that Bible, and she said yes. I shoved the paperback Bible into her travel bag.

Many of the people I was having these conversations with were thinking, "He is the guy who used to get drunk with us." It scared them. They acted the way people do when they're confused or ignorant of the facts.

When Jesus was with His disciples in the upper room the night before He died, He told them, "I am the true vine, and My Father is the gardener. He cuts off every branch in Me that bears no fruit, while every branch that does bear fruit He prunes" (John 15:1–2). The Father was about to do some drastic pruning in my life, and, boy, did it hurt.

CHAPTER 12

Change Can Be Painful

At a major management meeting in Memphis in 1977, IBM announced great bottom-line results and expansion plans. Promotions and accolades were lavished on many of my colleagues around the country—but not on me. Everything I had done right was minimized. I felt humiliated.

At a coffee break, I stood against the wall for support, and the Lord sent an angel to me to keep me from breaking down. Bill O'Toole, a big Irish guy, came up beside me and said, "Chris, what you did for me is so much bigger than what is going on here." I had shared Christ with him some months earlier.

That night my boss called my room and asked to see me. "Chad, what happened?" I asked him. "I had some of the best numbers in the country."

"Chris, nobody has the guts to tell you, but it is this Christ business," he said.

I felt like I'd been punched in the gut, the wind was knocked out of me. I was too immature to realize that the Lord had different plans for me, plans to prosper me beyond my wildest expectations. "'For I know the plans I have for you,' declares the LORD, 'plans to prosper you and not to harm you, plans to give you hope and a future'" (Jeremiah 29:11).

My career with IBM was effectively over.

Terribly upset, I called my mentor, Dick Woike, in Philadelphia. He gave me some Psalms to read, and they got me through the night. Jesus used the Psalms to help Him sustain the pressures and temptations of His ministry. When Jesus cried out from the cross, "My God, my God, why hast thou forsaken me?" He was meditating on Psalm 22:1–2.

For the next eighteen months I studied, prayed, and asked the Lord to guide me in my career. The Lord kept His promise: "Trust in the LORD with all your heart and lean not on your own understanding; in all your ways submit to Him, and He will make your paths straight" (Proverbs 3:5–6). Supernaturally, the Lord gave me peace and the grace to stay motivated, to serve the company that had done so much for me for the past ten years.

It did take a while for me to get to that point, I admit. I had my ladder against the wrong wall, but it hurt just the same when I was knocked off the ladder. I spent the time developing a life and career plan. I was thirty-seven years old, and I had gotten this far in my life with a lot of natural drive and a Swamp Yankee stubbornness.

Also, the Lord gave me a real break. He gave me Suzanne as a partner. She made all the difference with her support and encouragement. "Chris, you are my best friend. I think you are brilliant." She never really liked the whole IBM/IT culture. But now it was time to approach my life and career much more intentionally and with the help of God's guidance.

CHAPTER 13

Time to Leave

On May 22, 1978, I got off the train and walked into my boss's office. "Neal, I've come to realize you can run this company without me," I told him.

"Would you leave?" he asked, sounding surprised.

The reason he asked that is because the Lord had been giving me the grace to be content, to work hard, even though I had no real future with the company. I was waiting on the Lord for his guidance.

"Yes, if the package is right."

Two days later we met in a hotel room with my boss, Neal's boss from New York, a guy from HR, and an accountant. We cut the deal at the Latham Hotel in Rittenhouse Square in downtown Philadelphia. I had not quite reached ten years with the company. "Don't worry," they said. They were delighted to see me go. In fact, they were somewhat giddy. We met for two hours. They agreed to ten year vested rights even though I was six days short of the anniversary date of June 1, 1968, when I signed on with Big Blue.

I boarded the train and went home for lunch for the first time ever! Nobody at IBM went home for lunch. I was the only person in the railroad car. And I had a big check in my pocket. The sense of freedom was exhilarating.

I fasted and prayed for six days. I did not know how to fast—Jesus taught me. In the Sermon on the Mount, He said when you fast, not if you fast, implying you will. I went up to a third-floor spare room in our heavily mortgaged house with my Bible, a book on life planning, and a notebook. It was clear to me that evangelism was going to be my life's path, my calling. Whatever form it took, my mission would be to disciple men.

"Here am I. Send me!" (Isaiah 6:8). I wanted only to hear clearly from the Lord about where I was going next occupationally. Should I start my own company? He answered so clearly through His Word that I have never looked back, regardless of any difficulty.

With Suzanne in harmony, we applied for and were accepted into the ministry. We would join the organization Art DeMoss had started, Executive Ministries. I went that route because of the training opportunity it represented. I was now thinking strategically. I had to raise my own support, about $100,000 a year in the little town of St. Davids.

Ron Evans, the owner of a Christian bookstore, gave me a tool. "Go out and tell them what Paul wrote in Philippians 4:17: 'I don't desire a gift; I desire the fruit that will abound to your benefit.' Say the Lord called me into this work with business and professional people. I'm going to give you the opportunity to invest in it." It worked. Biblically, it is not begging, asking people to invest their discretionary dollars. The ideal was driving me internally.

Almost all the people I asked said yes. I ended up with about a hundred different people pledging, some as much as $100 a month. The local church was generous too. I learned that when you are raising money to support the work of the Lord, you will get what you need. I raised enough to qualify for Executive Ministries.

Suzanne and I decided to cash out of the house on St. Davids Avenue and found a smaller house in the nearby town of Berwyn, another fixer-upper. Suzanne paid the price of giving up her dream house, and for a while we had two mortgages. One month I could not make the payment on the new house and was going to lose the money we had invested in it thus far. That was weighing me down as I came out of the barber shop one night. I was trying to figure how to find $500 to pay the new mortgage.

Suddenly, a Buick pulled up, and the headlights hit me. Behind the wheel was my next-door neighbor, John Boyer, chairman of a company on the Main Line of Philadelphia.

"Chris, what is going on with you?" he asked. "You look terrible."

"John, I have to find $500 tonight or I'm going to be in a lot of trouble."

He whipped out his checkbook and wrote me a check. The Lord provided then and he has ever since. Some months later I was able to repay John.

While I was becoming more involved in Executive Ministries, its founder, Art DeMoss, dropped dead on a tennis court at the age of fifty-three. As we mourned him, Suzanne and I felt very vulnerable. We had sold the farm and joined a new organization. Now the heart of the work was gone with the passing of DeMoss.

During this time we sought professional advice from Howard Blandau, a professional counselor. Suzanne's and my communication and intimacy needed repair. It did not take very long for Howard to realize I was the one with all the baggage from the dysfunctional family and corporate bad habits. So Howard tried to help me get real, to tell the truth, to give of myself. With our two boys in the waiting area with coloring books, occasionally banging on the door, Howard masterfully led us into a deeper level of relationship.

One day when Howard saw me sliding back into my selfish and manipulative ways, he took the gloves off. "What is the matter, Chris, are you afraid we are going to find out who you really are?" He had pushed the right button of my self-deception: pretense. I felt so angry that I almost

Left: Campus Crusade (now CRU) founder Bill Bright; Right: Retired Col. Nimrod "Mac" McNair and wife Delysia came to lead Executive Ministries.

went over the desk to attack him. This was another critical turning point in Suzanne's and my relationship. We would go on to build on this for the rest of our lives together.

The year 1979 became a hard one. Things got political in the organization. Who was going to run it now? International headquarters began sending in people who did not have the necessary background. A ministry to business and professional people requires business and professional people.

Providentially an answer came from Bill Bright, founder of the worldwide evangelistic organization CRU, formerly Campus Crusade for Christ, which was the parent organization of Executive Ministries. Bright had a good friend in Atlanta, Nimrod McNair, a retired air force colonel, now running his own business and staying involved in Christian ministry. Bright asked McNair if he could take over Executive Ministries and he accepted.

What lay ahead now for Suzanne and me?

CHAPTER 14

Legacy of the Four

At Christmas 1980 I was forty years old. This seems a good place in this story for me to take stock. I had come a long way in life. Various people along the way had shown me kindnesses and patience. I had been able to bust out of generations of good people who loved me but did not have any vision of prosperity in the fullest sense.

The biblical vision of prosperity includes but is not confined to economics. The ideal was the Lord Jesus Christ himself. Luke wrote, "And Jesus grew in wisdom and stature and in favor with God and with man." With my conversion to the Christian faith in 1976, a whole new world began opening to me in all those dimensions: our relationship to God and to His people and wisdom. We were getting a whole new mind-set about purpose and meaning in life. It was late, but not too late. I was successfully emerging from my midlife crises.

Suzanne and I were part of a community, many of whom, like ourselves, were new in Christ. During this very special time of fellowship, Suzanne and I were close with four leaders and their wives who were exemplary in different dimensions of Christian service. You might even see them as gold standards in their respective focus of service. They became our mentors. So the four years between 1976 and 1980 were times of intense preparation.

Through those four men, I realize I had been given a gift, even a legacy. By their example, they modeled for me dimensions of an effective, superb Christian ministry. What I would end up doing in Atlanta was to emulate those talents myself with a team where we were able, with God's help, to develop people, especially men. God's unique calling on my life was beginning to take shape in my heart and mind.

These four men gave me the priceless legacy of showing faith in action with leadership.

The Wise Elder

Dick Woike, business partner of Art DeMoss and treasurer of National Liberty Corporation, was the wise older man, the elder. He was in his early seventies when I met him, and he had owned several businesses along the way. Some had even failed, but he saw failure as a great wisdom builder. He helped me to think through the many issues I had, coming out of darkness and into the light of the gospel of Jesus Christ.

Money and corporate politics were frequent topics of discussion. He was always there for me. He

Dick Woike

would rarely give me the answer to a problem but showed me the various tensions, different viewpoints in the Bible, which all point us back to trusting and obeying God. Dick was never judgmental, always patient, and personally supportive. He was a true mentor. A man with a wonderful sense of humor, he always taught the Bible with a smile.

He greatly admired Art DeMoss. One day he confided in me, "Art is so wise that he treats me like his father. He knows it would not work any other way."

In one Sunday morning Bible class, a Jewish couple who had come to know Jesus as their messiah wanted to make an issue about not eating pork. We were reading about the dietary laws in the book of Leviticus.

(Dick took us through the whole Bible in a year. He read it through, Genesis to Revelation, every year for fifty years.) Dick listened patiently and respectfully as he let the couple have their say. Then he said, "Okay, but all I want to say is that I still like my roast pork for Sunday dinner." He defused the tension with lighthearted humor.

The Bold Evangelist

Art DeMoss was the evangelist and a model for me. You might call evangelists the salesmen in the body of Christ. Every Thursday night for about two months we met at Art's carriage house for a study on marriage. He had recruited Bill Hogan to feed the fledgling Christians and those like myself who were not yet born again. Art etched something on my heart. He was an incredible archetype of a zealous witness of God's grace in his life. When Art died, Billy Graham, his friend, said DeMoss was the most effective personal witness he had ever met. Art would witness to God's grace to anyone.

Art DeMoss

Once on a trip to Washington with Art, I saw him challenge a presidential cabinet member who was a Christian. I will never forget that scene. Art looked up at the imposing politician, who was a foot taller than him, and admonished him, "You should be using your position to reach out to your community." Bold as a lion but gentle as a lamb, Art never employed any guile, which impressed me because I am a natural manipulator.

Art had built a relationship with the monsignor at the Catholic retreat center in Malvern, Pennsylvania, where various groups would come to retreat, including policemen, firemen, and schoolteachers. The monsignor gave Art the privilege of giving the final challenge at a Sunday morning service. Art, of course, shared his testimony and made the gospel of Jesus very clear. And then he gave a challenge for the participants to receive the Lord, to take the Lord to be their personal Lord and Savior. He would offer them a Bible if they would simply give him their name tag with an address. Before he died in 1979, he had given away ten thousand Bibles through that ministry at Malvern.

So, having heard about Art's generosity with his Bible ministry, in my immaturity I called him one day and asked him for a Bible. He was not effusive, but he said he would. Then I worried that I had been too aggressive.

One Thursday night at the carriage house study, he said, "Please see me afterward. I have something for you." He opened a big box that one of his secretaries had obviously packed for him. Tissue paper was flying everywhere. He sounded excited. "This is your study Bible. You will use this for preparing talks and studies. And this smaller Bible contains the New Testament, Psalms, and Proverbs. This you can carry with you and use when you counsel men and for your own enjoyment."

What was this genius doing? I might have just come to faith or been on the edge of faith, and already he was tangibly imparting to me a vision for a lifetime of ministry. It worked. That dear man marked me. He etched my soul. I will never forget Art DeMoss.

The Pastor/Teacher and Expositor

Bill Hogan was the Bible teacher and expositor at those Thursday night meetings. Interestingly, he was the teacher both at the Feminar where Suzanne met the Lord and at the Thursday night Bible study where I also received the Lord. Bill and his wife, Jane, had a long, rich background in Christian ministry.

After college, he had been on the staff of Campus Crusade for Christ and was involved in reaching out to young people principally on college campuses. Bill trained for a while under the tutelage of Dr. James Boice at a historic church in downtown Philadelphia. He went on to study at a seminary in Atlanta. Whenever he was teaching new converts, his text was always the Bible. What we saw and heard was an attitude toward the Bible that was intelligent and foundational to our lives and outreach to others. But more than that, he and Jane modeled the lost art of Christian hospitality.

He was the founding pastor of a new church in Wayne, Pennsylvania, a mile from our home in Saint Davids, with Sunday services held initially at a local high school. Every Sunday morning our two little guys, Christopher and Colin, and I would set up and tear down the chairs in the gym. My memory is that the Spirit of God was evident at that point in the history of the Church of the Savior.

When Bill brought a sermon of biblical exposition on Sunday morning, you could hear the pages rustling as many young, hungry Christians hung on his every word ("Like newborn babies, crave pure spiritual milk, so that by it you may grow up in your salvation" 1 Peter 2:2).

Bill Hogan

I remember so well the night Bill and Jane gathered several newly converted couples, including Suzanne and me, at their home for dessert. Bill said, "To start off, why don't we get better acquainted? Let's go around the room and share how our homes were heated when we were young."

Of course, I had a good story to tell about shoveling coal into the furnace as a boy. Bill's opening was a great example of hospitable fellowship that used something light and personal, an icebreaker, to help people start to connect. The example was not lost on Suzanne and me. The icebreaker became a key component of our small-group table-leader training and continues to this day.

As I started to grow in Christ and see the enormous potential for the kingdom of God in all these business and professional couples coming to faith, my "developer" talents led me to ask, "How does all this fit together?" So I asked Bill. I shared with him my curiosity, my questions. He quickly saw my curiosity as a calling to Christian leadership, and he suggested I think about seminary.

With the benefit of hindsight, I can see that the road I ended up traveling, catching graduate classes where I could in the summertime, was a better course. If I had taken Suzanne out of her situation with our two small children and relocated us to a seminary somewhere, all hell could have broken loose. It would be too much culture shock.

Bill was very reasonable though. When I later showed him the curriculum from the Institute of Biblical Studies, he conceded it might be the wiser choice. But he gave me a great challenge. He reached into his bookshelf and pulled down a book with study notes and cassette tape lectures by the father of the church growth movement, missiologist Donald McGavran. A missiologist studies how Christian missions work in various demographics and how it grows.

I devoured the course. There are certain patterns of growth in the body of Christ that can be observed, conceptualized, and taught. For instance, the gospel tends to move more rapidly in homogeneous groups (the homogeneous unit principle). That is why Art DeMoss was seeing such strong results. He was meeting the needs of business and professional men and women.

Another pattern is that the Holy Spirit is very creative. He will do different things in different ways because people are different. No cookie-cutter ministries, please. A lot of these phenomena make sense to pragmatic business people, but they might not take the time to read about them, articulate them, and discuss them.

I was getting the feeling that there was not enough conversation going on between the local church and the ministry of which Suzanne and I were more a part, with Art and Nancy DeMoss. Suzanne and I had been trained by the best of corporate America, IBM, and Federated Department Stores. We were used to working with highly competent leaders and managers. Communication is the lifeblood, the circulatory organ of any corporate system. The body of Christ is corporate. But, for a change, being low man on the totem pole and a volunteer, I kept my mouth shut.

My purpose here is to show you that Bill Hogan, like Art DeMoss, was a kingdom man. When he saw that I was becoming keen about the things of God, he took every opportunity to encourage me, to equip me with some of the vast resources that were available for men who seek first the kingdom of God. We need more men!

The Astute and Tireless Professional

Dave Balch, an attorney from the Midwest, and his wife, Dianne, had moved to the Main Line of Philadelphia for the express purpose of helping Art and Nancy DeMoss. There was no end to the work of following through with the new converts to the kingdom of God through Executive Ministries. After leaving his law practice in the Midwest, Dave and Dianne had raised the necessary funds and were full-time workers in the harvest field.

Dave was a professional, biblically astute and well educated and just as astute socially and relationally. He and I started to meet regularly. We called on men who had checked commitment cards at dinner parties and indicated they wanted to know more

Dave Balch

about a personal relationship with Christ.

This was my sweet spot. I was starting to apply the consultative skills I had acquired—essentially listening—to the work of one-on-one evangelism and the discipleship of men. And I was starting to do it more and more intentionally. This would be the training-wheels experience I needed for the work that God was preparing me for later in Atlanta.

Dave represented that intentional, professional approach necessary to keep the process moving forward and penetrating the culture. He was organized and tireless in his work with men. Dianne was right by his side, being very intentional in helping Suzanne grow. We became friends and even took some time together at the beach.

One day Dave and I called on an attorney in downtown Philadelphia. We had some time and merely stopped by his office. Dave said that he was there in connection with a dinner party this lawyer had attended at Laurier. He asked if he had any questions or concerns.

The man, though, had never been to a Laurier dinner party, which could have made for an awkward scene. But Dave was smooth, and before we left, he had shared God's plan of salvation. The man was polite but expressed a clear disinterest. Paul wrote to the Ephesians, "Be very careful, then, how you live—not as unwise but as wise, making the most of every opportunity, because the days are evil" (5:15–16). Dave made the most of this opportunity.

He was a tireless example to me. I ended up playing a similar role to his in Atlanta.

Through the ministry of these four men, Suzanne and I would be ready for the Lord to transplant us. That was coming!

CHAPTER 15

"Go for It": 1980, Philadelphia to Atlanta

The future for Suzanne and me would be decided at a meeting with Col. Nimrod "Mac" McNair, who had taken on the leadership role for Executive Ministries. To get away from all the tumult we were feeling in our lives, we held the meeting in Colorado in 1980 and came to terms with our role in the work going forward.

Suzanne and I agreed to move with the whole Executive Ministries operation to Atlanta, where Mac lived. At the Colorado meeting, Mac asked me to head up a training program. This fit with my background and talents.

Suzanne encouraged me, as always. "He is a big thinker," she said of Mac. "Go for it."

Fasting, prayer, and good counsel affirmed our decision. Then Pastor Bill Hogan, a staunch ally and friend, confirmed us for the work at the Church of the Savior with a small commissioning ceremony.

In late 1980 we prepared for our move. Logistically, it was quite an adventure. We met as a family, all four of us; Christopher was seven at the time and Colin was six. We asked the Lord to find us a new home. Suzanne flew down alone to see about the schools for our boys. They were at Delaware County Christian School in Philadelphia, and we wanted to continue training them in accordance with the will of God. Suzanne found the Heiskell School in Atlanta, and we knew that was where our sons would go.

———————

Suzanne and I agreed to move
with the whole Executive
Ministries team to Atlanta.
Mac asked me to head up
a training program. This fit with
my background and talents.
Suzanne encouraged me,
"Go for it." Fasting, prayer,
and good counsel affirmed
our decision. In late 1980
we prepared for our move.

———————

Now, for a house. We sat down and listed our criteria. We all had our preferences. The boys said, "We want to be near a ball field." We compiled a good list together and gave it all to the Lord in prayer. Finding our new home was my job.

We had enough money for one more plane ticket to get me to Atlanta. I arrived in the sunny South in December 1980. It was beautiful after the icy gray winters in Philadelphia, but it was still cold, and I was fighting the flu.

My father-in-law was in the real estate business in Connecticut, and he was part of a network with an Atlanta firm. A very inexperienced but lovely "willing to try" woman picked me up at an inexpensive hotel to show me several homes in our range. The critical criterion was the house had to be within twenty minutes of the Heiskell School.

Late that morning we came to a house on Dogwood Valley Drive. It took me a little while to realize it, but I knew it was for us, and we have lived there ever since. Two fireplaces. The kitchen was what we needed, and there were enough bedrooms. Yes, the house needed some updating, but we were a sweat-equity couple. I saw the vision, and this was the fourth and final house we renovated.

I told the agent to walk around the neighborhood and look for some Big Wheels. She came back with a good report. I went out in the backyard toward a clump of trees with the ground covered with pine straw and pine cones. I looked back at the house with the two flagstone patios on two levels and saw all of the possibilities. And downhill from our backyard was the ball field! I knelt in the pine straw under those big, beautiful Georgia pines and worshiped and thanked the sovereign God. He has provided for all those years, He is providing, and He will provide. He promised us in his Word, "Seek first His kingdom and His righteousness, and all these things will be given to you" (Matthew 6:33).

On New Year's Eve 1980, I was back in Philadelphia, standing in the yard of our home, which had sold easily—more providential care. I prayed to God about our need for money for the move, and at that moment Herb Rorer pulled into the driveway. Herb was an heir to the Rorer Chemical empire, makers of Maalox. He was a wonderfully generous personality whom we had reached for Christ through Executive Ministries.

Herb exclaimed, "Chris, I have just been with my accountant. He told me that today I have to give ten thousand dollars away to a not-for-profit

The Atlanta skyline in 1980, with the Interstate connnector under construction.

charity, and you came to mind." God is not cheap! The Lord was putting the whole package together for us: the school, the house, and the money for the move. I bought a used Chevy for five thousand dollars and found a mover to move us to Atlanta for five thousand dollars.

A month later Suzanne saw the house for the first time, and the powder-blue shag carpeting had to go. So the two little boys and I dragged the carpeting out of the house, through the front door, and exposed the beautiful hardwood flooring just as the moving truck was coming around the corner. Talk about living on the edge of faith!

CHAPTER 16

"Leave Your Guns at the Door"

The move to Atlanta came about through an innovative plan created by Nancy DeMoss, Colonel McNair, and CRU founder Bill Bright, an inspiring visionary who had launched ministries all over the world.

Bill Bright was a powerful leader and preacher. When I first heard him speak on the Great Commission—"Go and make disciples of all nations, baptizing them in the name of the Father and of the Son and of the Holy Spirit, and teaching them to obey everything I have commanded you" (Matthew 28:19-20)—I was so moved I thought I would explode!

The plan was to put together a team in Atlanta to take the model of Executive Ministries developed in Philadelphia and spread it all around the country. Some members of the team would focus on recruiting hosts for dinner parties in various cities. The start-up had been under way in Philadelphia before Art DeMoss died suddenly.

My job would be the role Dave Balch, my mentor, had filled as the full-time staff member who coordinated activities and kept the ministry on track. There were many others who helped me prepare for the work ahead, sometimes in seemingly minor ways. That was the case when I went to lunch with Dr. Bruce Wilkinson, the founder and president of Walk Thru the Bible Ministries. I met Bruce when he, too, had children at the Heiskell School.

Early on in Atlanta, I organized a breakfast meeting for the fathers at the Heiskell School. I encouraged them to bring a friend who did not know Christ. I asked Dr. Lloyd Stevens to give his testimony. Dr. Stevens, a prominent Philadelphia doctor who had been through the DeMoss dinner party ministry, was soundly converted, and his testimony was fresh, articulate, and powerful.

Bruce Wilkinson attended the breakfast meeting and suggested we get together. At lunch, we found we had a good rapport, and Bruce was empathetic. I shared with him how different the spiritual atmosphere was in Atlanta from that in Philadelphia.

Bruce seemed to be in harmony and he said, "Part of your problem is that you are a seminal thinker." I looked it up. A seminal thinker is a mind that opens new pathways for the minds that follow. Bruce had given a name to a pattern that was true about me.

I was made to create systems for marketing and selling intangibles, whether that be with IBM, where I was pivotal in new product marketing strategy and sales training, or Executive Ministries, the enterprise God had called me to, and the ultimate intangible: the gospel of Jesus Christ. I was called to create a new way to reach business and professional men for Christ in urban America. And I met my match in Atlanta. The city was ripe for some novel strategies. I worked to adapt the Philadelphia model to this new mission field.

In Atlanta, we met Jim and Ida Bell, a prominent couple who extended their hand of friendship to us. They became strategic partners for us in the development of the mission. They were open to the idea of being a host couple for the Executive Ministries evangelistic dinner parties in Atlanta. The Bells teamed with two other outstanding couples, Chris and Cynthia Carson and Brannon and Judy Lesesne. Chris was a highly respected partner with the Jones Day law firm. Brannon's business interests were Lesesne and Company Investment Advisors and Patterson Funeral Home.

Ida and Jim Bell

We worked the dinner party strategy, hosting dinners at the Cherokee Town Club in Buckhead and at the Capital City Club in Brookhaven. Both were upscale venues that provided nonthreatening settings for effective evangelism. For the follow-up appointments, I arranged to meet with men who had attended a dinner party. The model that Art and Nancy DeMoss developed in Philadelphia proved to be exceptionally effective in Atlanta.

Among the early converts were Jim O'Hanlon and David Butler, thinkers who, after some training in the faith, loved the Lord and committed their time, talent, and treasure to God's kingdom work. I met weekly with them and a couple of other men for fellowship in the corner of a restaurant.

The success of our work stemmed from Mac McNair's management style. He was a big thinker, as Suzanne had

Cynthia and Chris Carson

pointed out when we decided to move to Atlanta. He was also, to my surprise and delight, open to discussing the philosophical and conceptual basis for various strategies, which helped our relationship.

I start with philosophy. When my mind agrees conceptually, then I work tirelessly. Some people are more procedural, more process oriented. That is not good or bad; it is just one of the many ways that people differ. In the world of evangelism, discipleship, and pastoral leadership, an understanding of these matters is critically important. This was a good situation for me.

Mac was a management consultant and a teacher, but he had other sources of income, namely, business investments and his air force retirement. He was older than I and had "outgrown the pretenses of youth," to quote Matthew Henry, a sixteenth century Christian pastor. And the pièce de résistance of this strategic move to Atlanta: Colonel McNair was totally laissez-faire in his management style. So now I had a base of in-

Atlanta became the next chapter for our growing family.

come and the freedom to study, learn, and experiment. Nothing teaches more than on-the-job experience. That is true for all nonacademics.

God used our move to Atlanta to provide an ideal occupational motivational fit for me. The combination of my seminal mind and the freedom to experiment was perfect.

Yes, perfect for me, but how about Suzanne? Women often carry most of the load when their husbands make moves based on a sense of calling. The biggest factor in our success was Suzanne's partnership. She was willing to make the necessary sacrifices, because she knew this was God's will and plan for our lives. She was an obedient woman of God! When a man has a wife who admires him, who lifts him up and supports him, he is powerful. That is what Suzanne did for me.

Suzanne had a wonderful friend in Philadelphia, Patsy Fraser. Patsy and her husband, Ron, had come to Christ about the same time we did, and that gave us a common bond. We would have regular fellowship together, and we had what Ralph Waldo Emerson called the "bond of common experience." Suzanne and Patsy were nuts about home decorating. I mean, if you turned on the TV in our house, 95 percent of the time it was tuned to the Home channel.

Patsy and Ron were in a different financial class than Suzanne and I. It made no difference. Ron's father had been the chairman of Shell Oil

Company. Ron was a North-east classic, having received his education at St. Paul's School in New Hampshire and Princeton and Harvard Business School. He was now in the advertising busi-ness. Ron and Patsy were totally down to earth. All of us loved Christ and were growing together in Christ.

Ron and Patsy Fraser with Nancy DeMoss

Suzanne had a beautiful best friend in Patsy. Parting with her and Ron was one of the hardest things about our move. I point this out as another example of the sacrifices Suzanne made to follow our calling to Atlanta.

For my part, I had developed a close friendship in Philadelphia with Warrington B. McCullough III, or Tony, as we called him. Tony was part of my first table as a table leader when we were in Philadelphia. We be-came friends, and in that fellowship, Tony came to faith. I was rather

new in the faith, so we were growing together. When I joined the staff of Execu-tive Ministries in Philadel-phia, Suzanne and I decid-ed to liquidate the sweat equity we had at Saint Davids and move to a more modest home in Berwyn— another fixer-upper. All the shrubbery was overgrown,

Suzanne with Patsy Fraser

so Tony came over one day, and he and I had a marvelous day of fellow-ship while we tore out some plants with a chain hooked up to my Gran Torino station wagon. Two years later we moved to Atlanta and made a little money when we sold that house.

Left: Tony McCullough at Pine Valley Golf Club in his Pine Valley blazer;
Right: Anne and Tony McCullough

Tony, a championship golfer, has won several club championships at the legendary Pine Valley and Merion Golf clubs. Those courses are privately owned, and the "by invitation only" requirement to play there is a great prize for real golfers. Several times Tony has hosted groups from our Atlanta ministry to play at Pine Valley and Merion. He is all golf, and the men have enjoyed all of his tales about these legendary golf courses. Over the years those trips have contributed $200,000 to the ministry.

Tony and his wife, Anne, remained good friends to Suzanne and me. We have enjoyed trips to Nantucket and Long Boat Key, Florida, with them over the years. We have great fellowship because we all are focused on the things of God.

CHAPTER 17

Getting Started in Atlanta

One of the best examples of the dinner party strategy was an evening with Tom Hamilton, a renowned attorney from California. Jim Bell, a real estate developer and one of the hosts, introduced Tom and gave a short biographical sketch, including his impressive credentials, service on various boards, and other pertinent information. Incidentally, to avoid false expectations, the written invitation included the news that "Mr. Hamilton will also share his recent encounter with Jesus Christ."

Tom described how his life had been absorbed by his legal practice and his involvement in business investments and civic affairs. This imbalance left him estranged from his wife and family, and the pain he felt brought him to the place where he was open to the gospel. A colleague led him to Christ. He closed his story dramatically by telling how his entire family had responded to his changed life and they were reconciled. The family had surprised him at Christmas with a full-course dinner they brought to his home. There was not a dry eye at the Capital City Club dinner that night.

Jim O'Hanlon was one of the guests at the Tom Hamilton dinner party. Jim is married to Claudia, and he had been raised a Catholic in Maine. He was a Naval Academy graduate who had entered the famous Adm. Hyman Rickover Nuclear Submarine Program. He had served on nuclear submarines before leaving the navy and then worked in nuclear power consulting in Atlanta.

For the follow-up, Brannon Lesesne and I met Jim for lunch. It was a comfortable business lunch atmosphere, and I casually went through the FIRE process (family, interests/work, religious background, and experience of coming to know Christ) that I described earlier. Jim was amazingly transparent. I asked him where he was on his spiritual pilgrimage, and he told us how he had been searching. He had read Augustine's Confessions and had tried to read the Bible. The Lord gave us the privilege of working with Jim as God called him to Himself.

Brannon and I were grateful for the privilege of helping Jim. I asked him if he had read *The Four Spiritual Laws*. He had not, so we went through the booklet together. Before our lunch was over, Jim, without hesitation, humbly bowed his head and prayed to receive Christ that day.

The Four Spiritual Laws consists of four fundamental biblical truths:

1. God loves you and offers a wonderful plan for your life.
2. Man is sinful and separated from God. Thus he cannot know and experience God's love and plan for his life.
3. Jesus Christ is God's only provision for man's sin. Through Him, you can know and experience God's love and plan for your life.
4. We must individually receive Jesus Christ as Savior and Lord; then we can experience God's love and plan for our lives.

The little booklet was written by Bill Bright and has been translated into every major language. More than three billion copies have been printed. You can find an online version at 4laws.com.

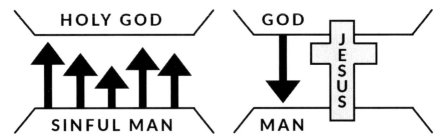

Man is sinful and separated from God, so we cannot know Him personally or experience His love. Romans 3:23, Romans 6:23, 2 Thessalonians 1:8-9

Jesus Christ is God's only provision for man's sin. Through Him alone we can know God personally and experience God's love. Romans 5:8, John 14:6

Concepts such as sin and Christ's atonement, repentance, and the role of our will in our salvation are made clear. We are saved by the grace of God, but God does not force us to choose Him. We must receive Him. "Yet to all who did receive Him, to those who believed in His name, He gave the right to become children of God" (John 1:12). According to *Strong's Concordance,* the original Greek meaning is "We must receive or take the gift." I cannot count the times I have parsed that verse over the years for men.

On this point we need to appeal more to the masculine mind. Not always, but men tend to respond better to facts and to challenge.

David Butler, another attendee at the Tom Hamilton dinner, was an attorney for a highly respected law firm in Atlanta and a former president of the Atlanta Bar Association. He was supportive, active in

One of Suzanne's beautiful paintings

the downtown YMCA, and an avid basketball player—a tall man and a real man's man. Later, he would develop his speaking skills. Along with many others in our ministry, I came to love his command of the Scriptures and his smooth, Southern, statesmanlike delivery.

Born in the South, David had grown up surrounded by, actually haunted by, Christianity—a term used by Ralph C. Wood in his study of a famous Georgia author, titled *Flannery O'Connor and the Christ-Haunted South.* David was now developing a more personal relationship with Christ.

As part of our Atlanta ministry, Ida Bell arranged coffees and Bible studies for the women. Suzanne always played a supportive role and followed up with the women personally. I am not sure what dinner it was that Sherri Johnston attended, but after one of these dinners, Suzanne followed up with Sherri. They developed a deep, personal relationship together for the next thirty years.

Sherri developed into a true woman of God, and she was instrumental in training women all over the world. One mission where Sherri had a big impact is called Women in the Window, a training ministry for women in the 10/40 window (a band of primarily Muslim countries, approximately 10 to 40 degrees latitude above the equator). When Sherri's husband, Tim, died prematurely, she spent more time traveling and discipling women. And then she met John Gorman.

One day Sherri and John asked me to lunch. I had no expectations of our get-to-gether other than a friendly meal, but they interviewed

Here I am officiating the marriage of John and Sherri Gorman.

me as a candidate to officiate their wedding. I am ordained by the Evangel Ministerial Association. I passed the test. What fun I had taking the traditional church wedding ceremony and adapting it to a simpler country-club setting. I made a lot of errors in my attempt to counsel them before the wedding, and I learned not to assume too much. The widow and widower taught me some great lessons. I learn everything the hard way.

Complicating our situation as we served on the Executive Ministries staff, Suzanne had almost no discretionary income. The generous Heiskell School family, Jim and Miriam Heiskell, gave us very helpful partial scholarships, but still the going was tough. Suzanne was tough, too! None of what we would develop over the next three and a half decades would have happened without Suzanne to back me up. She has been the back-bone of the whole enterprise: marriage, family, and business.

Early on in Atlanta, Suzanne was a part of a ladies' Bible study and other functions at some of Atlanta's lovely Southern homes. When she returned to our palace on Dogwood Valley Drive, she would almost sob. She was not envious, but she was an aesthete, and she did not have any resources. So the Swamp Yankee and his New York Seventh Avenue buy-er-wife started to get at it. Sweat equity is cheap! Suzanne painted all the outside brickwork on the house and bought a few canvases and created paintings of her own for our house. Her idiosyncrasy was that she only painted something when she needed a piece of art for a particular wall. I am biased, but her paintings are quite good.

CHAPTER 18

Wineskins

Now, I was splitting my time between helping to spread the dinner party concept nationally and developing a model ministry in Atlanta. In my mind these two facets of my work were inextricably connected. More and more I became interested in anything, any book, any serendipitous conversation that dealt with relationships for reaching and training God's people.

For most men, their only option is to be in a classroom or a pew where someone who is a whole lot smarter is teaching them. But what I had experienced in my years at IBM in consultative marketing and sales, and in my work in Philadelphia with Dave Balch and Executive Ministries, is that men respond better when the environment is smaller, more personal. Involvement and discussion are key. Men need to be participatory, more of a partner in their own growth. It is not too different from helping a business client to identify his business issue by having his consultant ask questions to uncover his needs. The process called the "guided group discussion" does just that.

Most relevant, the first-century church used the synagogue model of heads of households meeting together regularly. Ten men would hold each other accountable for the well-being of their families and also be accountable for their roles in the wider community. The Lord was leading me in this direction. The overriding issue: leadership!

In Howard Snyder's 1975 book *The Problem of Wineskins*, he proposed the thesis that the small group is a better wineskin, a better structure for the growth of people. See that "no one pours new wine into old wineskins… No, they pour new wine into new wineskins" (Mark 2:22). Jesus teaches through this story that the structure of the enterprise affects the effectiveness of the enterprise. This emphasis on the small-group structure was God's grace helping me to adapt the Philadelphia model to the Atlanta market.

I was starting to gain insights into some of the challenges of institutionalized churches. Training was important. And if I wanted to continue developing a public ministry, I would need more formal training to learn from men with more experience and biblical knowledge. There is a special dynamic of learning, of growth, when you are around a great scholar. Bill Hogan pushed this point on me in Philadelphia and encouraged me to attend seminary. But I would have to get this exposure in a different way.

We had begun to take advantage of a wonderful resource for training: the Institute of Biblical Studies (IBS). The parent organization of Executive Ministries sponsored an institute at Colorado State University in the cooler, drier Rocky Mountains. Every summer for seven summers we loaded the boys into the Chevy and spent a month there. We would rent an apartment off campus, and there would be a program for the boys. The Poudre River was nearby, and I vividly remember the swims in the cold mountain water with our boys. These are a special memory.

Top professors from evangelical seminaries around the country would teach two-week or four-week graduate-level courses. Three of these men impacted me particularly. Howard Hendricks, a professor at Dallas Theological Seminary and the chaplain of the Dallas Cowboys and president of the Leadership Center in Dallas, gave me the practical process for discipleship that I needed and implemented in Atlanta.

Walter Kaiser, a PhD in Semitic languages from Brandeis University and an Old Testament scholar and academic dean at Trinity Seminary in Chicago, captured my heart with his love and enthusiasm for the Scriptures, especially the Old Testament. He was

Dr. Walter Kaiser, PhD

such an effective teacher that in a class on the Pentateuch with two hundred to three hundred students, I earned a top grade. I passed this training onto the men in Atlanta by teaching them the Ten Commandments, Ecclesiastes, Ruth, Jonah, Malachi, and other books of the Old Testament.

Dr. John Hanna, from Dallas Theological Seminary, was our professor of church history—a topic some have called the "Third Testament." I assign to any man who wants to read it and who I think can

Hundreds of leadership lessons spanning over 20 years are available via online audio and video at leadmin.org.

handle it, *Church History* by Bruce Shelley. Church history gives leaders context. Battles they are fighting have been fought by men for more than two thousand years. Control and hubris, in men especially, has caused God's people to forget who said, "I will build My church, and the gates of Hades will not overcome it" (Matthew 16:18). When we try to build His church, we screw it up.

Suzanne, with her steel-trap mind, also took courses with me, and we would talk the whole lesson through. We were a great team. Walter Kaiser changed my attitude toward Suzanne and our marriage with his exposition of this one single truth: "The LORD God said, 'It is not good for the man to be alone. I will make a helper suitable for him'" (Genesis 2:18). The word helper, Kaiser explained, is the same word used when the Bible refers to God as our help and strength. So, Dr. Kaiser asked, "What kind of person is able to help someone?"

Yes! Our stronger wives are with us to help us and even to show us the way, albeit without usurping our role in the family. Eliza Pinckney, a friend of George Washington's, said to her father, who was concerned about her getting married because of her strength of personality, "Father, do not worry, he has his province and I have mine." That kind of wisdom can change the world.

Through Dr. Kaiser's profound teaching, my wisdom grew. IBS was just what the doctor ordered to build my confidence in the Bible. In addition to being under these three great scholars, probably the most strategic course was on hermeneutics by Professor Dick Purnell. Hermeneutics is the technical term for how to study the Bible. The key principle is context. A text out of context is a pretext.

Before I leave our experience at IBS, I must share with you a wonderful surprise I had while taking a course on world missions. The assignment was to do a research paper on a historically significant missionary. So I went to the religious research section at the Colorado State University library and rummaged through the sparsely stacked shelves. There, on the end of a steel shelf, sitting all alone and covered in dust was a large green volume on St. Patrick. Do you mean to tell me there is more to Patrick than green beer on March 17? Yes!

What I discovered in preparing that research paper and my subsequent studies is that since the missionary journeys of the apostle Paul, there is no greater missionary of the gospel of Jesus Christ in history than Patrick of Ireland. In the tradition of Paul, Patrick was called by God to suffer for the gospel. And Patrick wrote that for thirty years he thought he might die every day, given the resistance he faced from the pagan druid priests.

I subsequently developed a brochure titled *Lessons in Leadership from Saint Patrick*. Over the years, we printed hundreds of these brochures. The men and I used them in our ministries. Ted Shelling, a zealous missionary colleague, carried these brochures with him in his international travels. Patrick is another part of church history who has been clouded by misinformation and superstition. Given the many copies of the brochure we printed and its availability on the Leadership Ministries Inc. website, some man somewhere opened his heart to the Lord after reading the truth about Patrick. I look forward to meeting Patrick someday in heaven.

At this point in the early 1980s, when I was still formulating my convictions and strategy, I had a bright idea that I could be a force for change in the strategic city of Atlanta. I would do this by going where the power brokers congregated and by helping to revitalize these leaders spiritually. I could help change the world!

My idea was driven mostly by inexperience and ambition. I had more lessons to learn. A leader of a mainline church approached me and asked

Through Patrick's work, Ireland experienced the grace of God in every corner of the land. Thousands of Irish pagans accepted Christ as their Lord and Savior. Leaders were trained and churches were established.

The Irish church sent out missionaries to other parts of Europe becoming a European educational center.

Before his death, the whole country had come under a biblically based legal code.

LEADERSHIP LESSONS FROM SAINT PATRICK

me to be on his evangelism committee. Now this was something I knew about. After all, I had been trained by the best, Arthur DeMoss, whom Billy Graham described as the most effective personal witness he had ever met.

I attended the committee meetings, though I had never done well with committees. When I understood these committees defined evangelism as getting people to join the church, I had an emotional reaction. It upset me. I was shocked by their abject ignorance of biblical evangelism, and I knew I was in the wrong place. I gracefully bowed out lest I get myself in trouble.

Evangelism does not work that way. To evangelize, you first need to make the gospel clear to people who do not know the Lord. You go where they are. The gospel of Jesus Christ is founded on the fact that God gave His only Son to save sinners. The gospel, the good news, is not about the church; it is about Jesus.

Dr. Ruth Ann Breuninger, a former college professor and career Christian education expert, asked me to teach a Sunday school class. This great open door gave me a place to learn how to teach what I was learning at IBS and how to use my new study tools in my own personal study. The class was full of older men and women who taught me a lot about Southern grace. I was too brash and would soon get my comeuppance.

Dr. Ruth Ann Breuninger

Nathan Moore had founded the class in 1937, and he was still there in 1982 when Ruth Ann threw me in there. I asked him if I could see him, and he invited me to his modest apartment, which was sparsely furnished and had linoleum floors.

"Chris, I have been promoted by the Lord. The only thing I have to do all day now is to pray," Nathan told me.

I should have taken the cue right there. I was with a special man of God, and I had better not fool around. But I had my agenda. I hemmed and hawed as I spoke to him about changing some things in the class.

"Chris," he said, "please be frank."

Those words cut me to the quick. I was dishonoring this older man with insincere manipulation, a sin. Another painful lesson. If lessons don't hurt, they don't do much. But we got through the meeting, and he was supportive of my suggestions. Suzanne and I taught that class for five years.

Later, Nathan expressed appreciation for my leadership, telling me that I was very "listenable" as a teacher. I would go on to develop that quality in my teaching, making it understandable and therefore "listenable." My inspirational support for this practice comes from several places in the Bible. One of my favorites is the book of Nehemiah: "They read from the Book of the Law of God, making it clear and giving the meaning so that the people could understand what was being read" (8:8). I thank God for Nathan and his ministry in my life.

Sundays began with Suzanne opening the class and breaking the ice with something light. Nathan recited one of his famous prayers, and I taught the book of Romans a paragraph at a time.

One of my older friends, Ellen Pope, discerned it was good for me and encouraged me to keep studying. Later, she brought me John Calvin's *Institutes of the Christian Religion.* Margaret Asbury brought me another treasure, *Explore the Book,* by J. Sidlow Baxter. These women were part of my septuagenarian fan club. Mature Christian women are wonderful! They are "wise as serpents and gentle as doves." Suzanne became one of these wise women. I treasure my memory of being their fledgling teacher. I love them all and look forward to seeing them again in heaven.

The United Class was the right place for Suzanne and me to serve as I was developing my theology and my philosophy of ministry. I burned the midnight oil every Saturday night as I prepared for the class, and then I saw Suzanne showing some signs of irritation. Was I pushing her too hard? I needed to have no worry. She was, as always, a rock of support. She would critique the lesson as we drove home via Peachtree Road. It often hurt, but I could take it because of my love and respect for her. I trusted her. "No pain, no gain."

This was a wonderful opportunity. I needed to develop my own convictions while developing the work of Executive Ministries. The desire to serve the Lord was a "burning fire shut up in my bones" (Jeremiah 20:9 KJV). I tried to visit with class members when I could, the big power brokers first. When I moved the conversation to personal salvation with one man, he reminded me he was an elder and shut down that line of conversation. Since we were in his downtown club, I politely steered the talk toward a less personal vein. That conversation made a big impression on me. He was hiding in the institution.

We stayed with the United Class for five years before the Lord moved us on. Suzanne was the Lord's catalyst. She was usually ahead of me on our timing, but I eventually caught up with her. She could see we had landed in a cul-de-sac from the main road of our calling.

I had another mind-altering experience when Suzanne and I attended a conference at Callaway Gardens and heard Stuart and Jill Briscoe, speakers with a worldwide teaching ministry. Stuart is an ordained pastor with a large church in Wisconsin. At this time, they were traveling and had given their lives tirelessly to kingdom service. Stuart had a repeated refrain wherever and whenever he spoke: "Mobilize, then motivate! Give men jobs!"

Bingo! That principle would become a cornerstone of my ministry philosophy going forward. When I heard it, I knew it was true. It totally fit me. I was made to mobilize men, especially business and profes-

Bob Day

sional men. But what would that look like? How would I get to that point?

Well, I believe you start with a man God sends your way. One such man was Bob Day, a real estate professional who visited the United Class with his wife, Marie. That began a forty-year friendship.

Years later Bob wrote: "It all started when Marie and I met you teaching our Sunday school class. One morning after class, I asked you a question, and you challenged me to read and research for myself. I took up your challenge, and that was the beginning of a long-term tutelage, friendship, and training relationship."

Bob also commented on how that challenge led to many others for the rest of his life, including the huge, vital roles he went on to play in the ministry to men. "Marie and I are so grateful for that small beginning at

As Baxter stated,
"Some persons… have got more knowledge and remorse of conscience in half an hour's close discourse, than they did in ten years of public preaching."

church," he said. "It changed the trajectory of our lives and we say, thank you, Chris and Suzanne!"

The Bible is clear, we are commanded to get together with other Christians for the purpose of encouragement and spurring each other on.

How can you spur one another on if you do not know the people, if you are not able to interact with them, know their needs, and pray for them?

On a vacation I was gripped by a book written 350 years ago by Richard Baxter, a Puritan pastor of a small congregation at Kidder Meister, Worcester, England. His work there among the rough, rural farmers and the others in the community, including those of the professional class, is considered a classic of pastoral leadership.

The aspect of Baxter's writings that caught my attention was his emphasis on personal interaction with the heads of families, whom he would develop by teaching them with literature that he provided. He was a highly disciplined man and made it his practice to visit each man in his parish at least once a year and give them some assigned reading and study. The following year he would check up on these heads of households. That was where Baxter's focus was. He did not spend undue time or reliance on his pulpit ministry. Instead, he focused on personal, one-on-one work with the men in the community. I took a modernized version of Baxter's book, *The Reformed Pastor*, and made a study guide out of it. Twenty men and I pored over this study guide for two years.

As Baxter stated, "Some persons… have got more knowledge and remorse of conscience in half an hour's close discourse, than they did in ten years of public preaching."

More than ever I knew one-on-one and small-group or table fellowship would be the wineskin I would develop. But at the same time, a new concept would open the door to the future for Suzanne and me.

A text out of context is a pretext.

CHAPTER 19

God's Talents—
"Coke Machines"

By 1985 I started to realize the skills, training, and growth I had gained over the past twenty years were preparing me for exactly what was needed in the Atlanta area: making real workers and leaders who were able to lead men to Christ and disciple them in the faith. My day job was ensuring the dinner-party strategy spread nationally, but my heart was centered on the local community, the local church.

In my role of developing the national strategy of Executive Ministries, I had some real success. Probably one of the biggest wins was equipping Pat Morley of Orlando, Florida, with the concept we were developing in Atlanta. Allen Morris was working the Executive Ministries model in Miami, and he introduced us. Pat came to Atlanta with a team for a two-day workshop. He returned home with the manuals that John Creamer, a gifted colleague, had helped to write, as well as some tapes. Pat went right into action.

This was the early incubation of Pat's Man in the Mirror Ministries. Pat is a true entrepreneur and a gifted leader and writer with great vision. His 1989 book *The Man in the Mirror* captured the imagination of men worldwide. He went on to be regarded as one of America's most respected authorities on the unique challenges and opportunities facing men. Through his speaking and writing, Pat is a tireless advocate for men, and his organization has helped to impact twelve million lives around the world.

———————————

The Bible is for living.
The Scriptures are alive and powerful. The Word of God can, and has, changed the world!
But hundreds of men sitting in church, not actively engaged, and discussing the Scriptures will not get the job done.

———————————

Years after Pat's visit to Atlanta, I received an email from a missionary in South Africa asking me for guidance. He had fifty men meeting in a restaurant and wanted some direction moving forward. Pat had selflessly equipped the missionary with the materials I had given him. We were privileged to have had the opportunity to invest in Pat Morley, this man of God, and his work.

The pastor of a large church called me and asked me to speak to his elders on a Monday night. He was a very humble man and said, "I am not sure what more I can say to these men." That was a tough night as forty elders listened stoically while I explained the need for leadership development as the product of all their organizational machinery and multi-million-dollar budget. My speaking there gave me a chance to experiment with communicating some of the convictions I was developing. I was becoming more and more convinced that, in and of itself, organizations were not going to do the job. Every enterprise needs good organization, but organization is not an end biblically. It's a tool.

When Paul wrote about organization in the body of Christ, his concerns were more descriptive than prescriptive. Also, Paul puts the focus for organizing around gifts and talents. Preachers should have gifts of prophecy and confront others with the truth. Pastor-teachers should exegete, or pull out, the truth and present the truth in a way that allows people to learn and grow.

The Bible is for living. The Scriptures are alive and powerful. The Word of God can, and has, changed the world! But hundreds of men sitting in church, not actively engaged, and discussing the Scriptures will not get the job done, no matter how busy the leaders get with church work. The work of the church is to make disciples.

More than ever, I was focused on reaching men in Atlanta.

The burden growing in me was somewhat subjective. It resulted from the lack of male spiritual leadership in my life as a child, which resulted in devastation in my life. I went into adolescence and puberty without even one conversation with a mature man about how to manage my new body. The result was a disaster. But the burden now was also growing because of my new understanding of biblical manhood.

For the average man in Atlanta, and for that matter everywhere else in the United States, the Bible is not a working tool for him to be able to lead in the primary institutions of marriage, family, and business life.

Dr. Richard Halverson

Senator Tip O'Neill of Massachusetts famously said, "All politics are local." So is all of God's work! But what is the locale of the local church?

Dr. Richard Halverson, chaplain of the U.S. Senate from 1981 to 1995, stirred my imagination during a visit to Atlanta, when he challenged a congregation of mainline churchgoers with this statement, "You are the church. The church is where you are."

Inspired by Dr. Halverson's challenge, I gave a message on Coke machines to some men at a Friday morning meeting.

I asked them, "Where does Coca-Cola put their Coke machines? Do they expect all of their customers to come down to their headquarters in Atlanta on North Avenue to buy a Coke? No, of course not. They put the machines where the people are, even in our own offices."

We are called to bring the gospel to men. I would try to use public restaurants for meetings while I was developing the model in Atlanta for Executive Ministries. When I met with Nathan Moore, a retired accountant and founder of the United Class whom I mentioned previously, I told him about our strategy of using restaurants.

"Chris," he responded, "I think you are reaching new levels of efficiency for the church!" More encouragement from Nathan. I got off on the wrong foot initially with Nathan, but I am thankful we finished well.

CHAPTER 20

Long-Term, Low-Pressure

By the mid-1980s we were starting to gain momentum. John Creamer and Steve Nichols, fellow staff members, and I combined to start regular Friday morning meetings. The work was taking form, reflecting the research I was doing on structure. Developing this idea in Atlanta was where my heart was, my brewing passion, and my effervescence was going to blow the cork off the bottle.

And then Bill Bright fired Mac McNair! They were friends, and Mac had always told me how much he admired Bill, a man of great vision. By the mid-1980s, Bill's organization had work going on all over the world.

Tucker Yates, a colleague, gave me a good picture of how visionaries operate. Think of them as driving a speedboat on a clear lake. All they can see in front of them is smooth sailing, but as they jam the throttle forward, the wake of the boat creates turbulence. Bill was the quintessential visionary. That was his gift. Mac was not moving fast enough and was in the way. At least, that is my guess. Bill and Mac are now together in heaven with the Lord, each receiving his "well done, good and faithful servant."

A wise man, Colonel Mac had played a key role for several years in allowing the work to develop by absorbing the pressure to go faster. For me, the motivational climate that allowed me to mature in Christ and develop my own philosophy of ministry was going to change.

Every corporate body has its own culture, its own personality. A high value in Bill Bright's world was production. When you have a vision for seeing God's Great Commission fulfilled within a few years, the implication is that you had better hurry. And the culture is impatient. But at the grass roots, I learned that more patient, long-term strategies were needed. I developed the slogan, "Long-term, low pressure."

There are no superheroes in the body of Christ. Every man who plays the role of husband, father, and business or professional experiences enormous pressure. Some men with private school tuitions, mortgages, club dues, etc. need to make a quarter of a million dollars before they can even put food on the table. Keeping up with the Joneses is exhausting.

I learned this empirically, on the job, by getting more closely involved with men, building relationships. Relationships take time. The currency for building relationships is trust, which comes slowly. The men in Atlanta had seen it all. Several evangelistic campaigns had been conducted in Atlanta over the years.

Even as I was moving toward long-term strategies, I was not immune to the desire to gain social status, illustrated by an incident involving my friend David Butler, who had been led to a walk with Christ early on. During the first year of our friendship with David, Suzanne and I received a box of Florida grapefruit from his prestigious downtown Atlanta law firm at Christmas. David was married to an award-winning photographer. That same Christmas we received the Butler family's card with a photo of his pretty wife and their five beautiful, high-achieving kids. When I received the fruit and the Christ-

David Butler

mas card, I said to myself, through my immature spiritual eyes, "White, you have arrived! You are being accepted by Atlanta's heavy hitters."

But it was only when I got to know David over the next thirty years that I came to understand his struggles and be the kind of friend

Small groups of men gathered around a table for discussion and development became the hallmark of our Friday morning meetings.

to him that he was to me. He was a great ally. When he later went through a painful divorce, he often visited with Suzanne and me, and we were able to help him bear the burden. He rented an apartment in our neighborhood to be close by. One night he said to us, "I am about to die." He trusted us and shared his pain with us. No man was more encouraging to me in the early days than David Butler. And he is with the Lord now.

Bill Bright's campaign "Here's Life, America" had blown through Atlanta in the 1970s. Converts from that campaign were now being absorbed into the organized church. Frank Strickland, a gifted business consultant, became a table leader for our Friday morning meetings. He was a natural, with an easygoing, relational style. He saw what I was trying to do.

By this time in our development, we were leading and managing twenty tables of men at three locations. I was meeting monthly with most of the table leaders, a group I called the First Cut Leadership Forum. The name is derived from the biblical idea of giving the Lord the first cut of the harvest or flock.

One Friday David Fritz showed up and sat at Frank's table. David was hurting so badly that he ended up venting and was disruptive.

Frank called me over and asked, "Chris, what should I do? I'm afraid that if I call him and invite him back, he will show up."

I was tempted to say, "Do not bother," but instead I said, trusting God, "Frank, we don't have a choice. You have to call him."

Frank called him, and for a while Dave was so needy and unruly that it

David Fritz

put enormous pressure on Frank. But that is what we do in Christian ministry. We rely on God to give us patience as we work with men. That is what Jesus modeled as he trained the Twelve. Can you imagine what an enormous task that was to turn these men into real disciples?

Dave had a bunch of difficult issues to deal with that came from divorce, mixed families, economic pressure, and more. Over a long period of time and through a patient, long-term, low-pressure strategy, Dave stabilized in the faith, led a functional family, and developed a successful financial planning practice.

When I first met Dave, he was selling mortgages, but I informally coached this former air force pilot and obviously gifted man with a keen mind to broaden his range of financial services. Eventually he became a financial planner and helped struggling, lower-middle-class men and women become middle-class millionaires. That's a great work!

Dave's story, like so many others, affirms the rewards of our mission. Like putting Coke machines in office buildings, bringing the gospel to men where they are in the marketplace was starting to pay off.

Discipleship is the greatest business in the world. It is hugely productive and offers eternal returns on investment. But—and this is important—it needs patient leaders who can work in a long-term, low-pressure environment alongside a patient, consistent group of faithful men who are growing, too. Not a nervous or busy culture.

CHAPTER 21

Up to the Mountain

The last ten years had been very good and extremely productive. Suzanne and I had grown in Christ, and we had increased our Christian training. But I felt I needed to be transplanted. I was feeling constrained working in the large corporate structure with its own political culture.

In the fall of 1986, I told my friend Bogue Miller I needed a place to get away. Bogue, a very resourceful real estate broker, was an emerging leader on Friday mornings. He was a faithful man at First Cut Leadership Forum meetings. Through his network, he gave me a key to a rural church campground cabin in a tiny place called Tiger, Georgia, about eighty miles north of Atlanta, near Lake Burton.

There, in a simple mountain cabin with the barest of necessities, supplied by cool spring water, in fasting and prayer, I searched for the way ahead. My talents as a business consultant had lain dormant in Executive Ministries. My study of the Scriptures had shown me that God wanted all the talents He has given me put to use. Think of the servant who received Jesus' coveted "well done, good and faithful servant! You have been faithful with a few things; I will put you in charge of many things. Come and share your master's happiness" (Matthew 25:21). He had put all of his God-given talents to work.

For days at that mountain getaway I worked through Solomon's Ecclesiastes, writing and praying earnestly, filling up the notebook I had brought with me and absorbing Solomon's wisdom and knowledge. The repeated refrain from Solomon about work was to enjoy your work and go about your business wholeheartedly!

I opened my heart to God: Lord, I love this work, but I feel like I have one hand tied behind my back. I am not wholehearted! I need guidance, Lord. Am I a missionary or a business consultant?

I was taking an advisory attitude with men, and I was seeing the fruit, the fruit that remains. "You did not choose Me, but I chose you and appointed you so

In the north Georgia mountains I found a spiritual retreat.

that you might go and bear fruit—fruit that will last" (John 15:16).

And then the answer came. Clearly. Yes, I should use my business consulting skills in concert with the work of evangelism and discipleship. A verse from Ecclesiastes lit up like a neon sign: "Sow your seed in the morning, and at evening let your hands not be idle, for you do not know which will succeed, whether this or that, or whether both will do equally well" (Ecclesiastes 11:6).

I was overcome with praise and thanksgiving to God for His generous mercy to me. He freed me up. I stopped at a small country store on my way home and bought a beer to celebrate. I came down off that mountain with God's permission slip to do the work He had prepared for me.

I would become a bi-vocational missionary providing service to the community through a not-for-profit ministry and a commercial business consultancy. Now the question to be answered was, "How do we do all this?"

CHAPTER 22

Open Doors

If we Suzanne and I were to spin out of Executive Ministries, money was going to become a major challenge. Our investors had signed up to support the work that we had come to Atlanta to develop, so communication with these individuals was very important. I made sure to stay close to them. Ninety-five percent of them stayed with us.

Suzanne was very positive about the potential for a change, and she had a look of determination that said, "You can count on me."

One weekend Suzanne and her friend Patty Renfroe attended the Center for Christian Concepts (CFC) in Gainesville, Georgia, led by financial planning guru Larry Burkett. After the weekend, Suzanne told me, "God has called us to this work of discipleship, but I do not want to be broke all the time."

Her approach was to be obedient to everything she had learned at CFC. So we cut up all the credit cards except one, which we used for travel. We made sure we gave generously to the redemptive work of Jesus Christ. We used the model my friend Robertson McQuilkin wrote about in his 1989 book, *An Introduction to Biblical Ethics*. He said to start giving legalistically at 10 percent, which was required under the Old Testament law. You can't make a case for this law in the New Testament, but McQuilkin suggested it was a good place to start for people saved by the grace of God. The Lord lays down the challenge in Malachi: "'Bring the whole tithe into the storehouse, that there may be food in my house. Test me in this,' says the LORD Almighty, 'and see if I will not open the flood-gates of heaven and pour out so much blessing that there will not be room enough to store it'" (Malachi 3:10).

Suzanne took that challenge. For the next three decades, the first thing she would do every month was to write checks to the various works we support. As soon as she finished writing the checks, she wanted me to bring them to the post office, no matter how long before pickup. It helps to be a little fanatical when you are developing a discipline such as giving. Our tax accountant even asked her if she might be overdoing it. She ig-nored his advice! God said, "Test me," and she did.

On the expense side, we developed a budget, and every Monday she withdrew the cash in preselected denominations and put the bills in her envelope system. She gave me an allowance in cash every Sunday night. If I had to use a credit card for any reason, I had better tell her that day or I would be in serious trouble.

Nothing was fancy, but it was faithful, consistent over a long term, and that helped to create peace and security in our home. Suzanne got to a point where she enjoyed saving money and giving money more than spending money. She kept her figure by diet and exercise and used some of the same clothes for decades. She always looked good. She was following the model preached by John Wesley, father of the Methodist movement: "Make all you can, save all you can, give all you can."

Her faithfulness in biblical money management and prayer was foundational to the development of our ministry going forward. Care-ful money management is foundational to any enterprise, especially the gospel ministry. I fully recognize that Suzanne's careful stewardship of our financial resources was one of the biggest factors in our survival and success going forward.

My time with the Lord became more intense. He was giving me patience. Pastor Jim Stevens had told me, "You are the steward of your gifts." Pastor Russ Cagle warned me, "Do not try to open your own doors. Wait on the Lord."

I was in the same place I had been eight years earlier when I knew it was over with IBM, but the path forward was not clear. I knew I was com-ing to a crossroad. A God-directed crossroad in His timing. God told me, "Chris, trust me. I have never let you down. I have kept every promise."

That was an evident truth for me, but economics was now a big factor in the mix of pressure points in my life. Pressures were growing on me as we were in the peak child-rearing years. Our sons, Christopher and Colin, teenagers now, were at Mount Vernon Christian Academy, and both were preparing to go to college. Pretty soon they would start driving, then college. More money, more fundraising. Pressure, more pressure!

My strategy was to provide a service worth supporting. I wanted men to personally experience our ministry. I am not good at singling out wealthy people to promote the organization, but some of that is necessary, of course. And I have done my share. At this point, though, I had to ask, "What organization?" There was none.

I do not know what the politics were for the decision to fire Colonel Mac. Several men had moved their families to Atlanta to join the development team, and Mac's wife, Amy, shared with me that Mac was taking that fact very seriously. The way she put it, he just sat in a chair for hours, thinking and praying. I think he was suffering from depression.

God kept opening the doors. I was at my sons' baseball game one night, standing behind the backstop at home plate, when I met Charlie Renfroe, Patty's husband. Charlie was an entrepreneur who started out cutting lawns as a young man and now had a good-sized company focused on outdoor billboard advertising and a data records storage company for law firms. Everything was profitable. Our sons were friends and played ball together.

Charlie and Patty Renfroe

We seemed to have a rapport. I invited him to join me on Friday mornings. Less than a month later, I asked him to be our emcee. From 1986 onward, Charlie served as our emcee when he was not at his farm, his home at the beach, or his mountain retreat. He enjoyed traveling in his Airstream with his grandchildren in some part of the country he had not been to before. Charlie is truly an amazing man. He taught himself to play the piano as an adult and has the uncanny ability to make a new man at FMMF feel at home. He has brought a wonderful dimension to our fellowship with his storytelling from his vast life experiences.

113

We branded the ministry to men in Atlanta the Friday Morning Men's Fellowship, and we were gaining traction, building momentum.

Another open-door example was the arrival of Ken Thrasher, who was sitting on the front porch with his neighbor, Bob Day, when Bob invited Ken to a Friday morning gathering. Ken and his partner, Rick Bennett, had built an accounting, tax planning, consulting, and wealth management powerhouse in Atlanta at Bennett Thrasher LLP. Ken is the penultimate financial professional. And he really cares about people.

Friday Morning Men's Fellowship (FMMF) met in an area restaurant. Bottom photo, left to right: Russ Neal, Jim Bennett, Mike Loia

Dave Dorries readies our clothespin nametags for Friday Morning Men's Fellowship.

Ken's involvement unexpectedly opened another door. He was working with a friend and client, John Spivey, who had built a circle of Bobcat dealerships that ringed the city of Atlanta. John was a big, burly, rough, tough guy with a teddy-bear heart. Ken extended his professional financial counsel to John's personal life and invited him to join us on Friday mornings. Charlie Renfroe, the emcee, kept the atmosphere safe, no institutional or cultural barriers to cross, only neutral ground.

John became a regular as well as a delightful friend. Our ministry was an incubator for his faith. I visited with him and tried to help him understand God's grace and forgiveness in Jesus Christ. He gave financially and was sympathetic to our economic challenges.

Eventually, I shared with John and a small group of men the realities of our financial picture. Listen to the following wisdom from a tough businessman who had experienced God's grace. "Chris, here is your problem," he said, "you are like the tutor who gets the student ready for his exams. The student goes up to the university, passes the exam, and the university gets the money—not you."

How would I be able to pursue my vision of reaching men and training them in the gospel given these economic realities? I faced the fact that I needed some staff. But the bigger issue for me was my style. I wanted to fund the ministry to men by serving them professionally. My conviction was that men would give generously if they were properly grounded in the faith. My mentor Howard Hendricks counseled me, "If you don't reach the man's wallet, you haven't reached the man."

But that would take time, and I wanted to be able to set the pace. I wanted to be able to turn the big valves of the culture. Hospitality, the welcoming of strangers, is of paramount importance to me. I dusted off some of the life- and career-planning tools God had used to lead me into this kind of work in 1978 when I left IBM.

I was waiting on the Lord. I told Suzanne, "We will leave Executive Ministries when God opens the door." We would both have to cling to God and each other. It was an especially close time for both of us.

CHAPTER 23

The Door Opens

At a conference in Colorado in 1985, I had a chance to talk about the work of Executive Ministries. A dynamic young financial professional approached me and asked if I would get in touch with him. God was about to open my eyes to some new possibilities through a relationship with Don Hughes. He and his colleagues in the mortgage banking business in Memphis were building a new company, First Mortgage Strategies Group. They wanted to leverage their skills in packaging mortgages for savings and loans (S&Ls) that were having liquidity problems in the mid-1980s.

While the average S&L executive at that time was not terribly sophisticated in the world of secondary markets, I was completely ignorant of them. It was a great revelation for me when, during a visit with Don, I learned what a basis point was: 1 percent of 1 percent or .001. If you are a mortgage banker who can package $100 million in mortgages into a mortgage-backed security on Wall Street, and you could negotiate a 100 basis-point fee, you could make one million dollars. Everything depended on being able to properly analyze the quality of each mortgage. This was Don's core proficiency. He was a genius with accounting techniques.

People like Suzanne and I, who faithfully paid our mortgage every month, are valuable assets. I never thought the local S&L would sell our mortgage. It actually hurt my feelings when I understood all this. It was a whole new world for me. Talk about naive!

But I did know a little about what people need in their work. Men like Don Hughes and I need to be in charge. My time in the navy, my ten years with IBM, my eight years with Executive Ministries, my knowledge of the Scriptures, and the great mentors I have had all those years gave me some skills. I was learning to manage myself and counsel others. I started to coach Don Hughes informally, and he was exceptionally responsive to my input.

He called me from Memphis and said, "Chris, is there anything you could do for us as a company? We all need the tools you have been teaching me: how to relate and communicate. We are all so different."

From that point, we planned a "relate and communicate" off-site retreat at a re-

Don and Marcia Hughes

sort in eastern Arkansas about a hundred miles from Memphis. Suzanne and I, Don and his wife, Marcia, and all of the employees of First Mortgage Strategies Group spent two days together.

I designed the weekend around the importance of good working relationships in a small company. Assuming a group has technical competence, if the relationships are right, there is almost nothing they cannot do. The converse is also true: relational conflict breeds stagnation. Work becomes drudgery.

When people are emotionally bummed out in business because of poor leadership, productivity can take a beating. An effective leader understands that people operate differently. Some people need a more encouraging environment. That was the case with Bill, a member of the First Mortgage team.

Don's keen insight into the nuances of financial deals resulted in some frustration and criticism of Bill, who was a broad-brush optimist. Bill was dying emotionally and motivationally, but he provided a vital function for the team. Don looked to another staffer, Howard, to manage the group's day-to-day activities, but Howard was a technician who had little interest in the people side of things. Howard got it right, however, when it came to making sure the computer models were working and so forth.

Others on the team, like Pam and Gene, were doing well because they were as loyal as the day was long. Don gave them plenty to do, which satisfied a lot of their needs.

The team members were all good people. During the weekend they started to understand each other, and I taught them how to communicate more effectively with each other. Don was eager to be a more effective executive. He was trying against all odds to be an "exceptional executive," as described in the writings of Harvard's Harry Levinson. The exceptional executive keeps in mind the feelings of people, because happy, loved people are more productive. (Assuming their competence in their work, of course.)

In our seminar, I taught Don and his team how to use "I" language. For example: "Don, when you talk over me in meetings, I feel demotivated to give this company my best shot."

The team members learned to not criticize, blame, or be defensive, but rather to just speak the truth. Telling the truth can be hard to do. It takes courage.

Dr. William Backus, in his 1985 book *Telling Each Other the Truth*, estimated, on average, people lie ninety times a day. All the people on the team professed faith in Jesus Christ, but like many, they left their faith at home when they went to work.

Believing "work is only where you go to make money" is a lie. Abraham Kuyper in his *Stone Lectures at Princeton University* circa 1898 made the following statement: "There is not a square inch in the whole domain of our human existence over which Christ, who is totally Sovereign, does not cry, 'Mine!'"

We have more to do on the job beyond earning a paycheck. In her essay "Why Work?" author Dorothy Sayers, a friend of C. S. Lewis, goes further by pointing out, "Our work is our worship."

In our relate-and-communicate sessions, we opened the eyes of the leader and the team. We could see the light bulbs going on. They loved the workshop, and Don and Marcia were very pleased.

On the way back to Memphis, Suzanne and I were in the backseat of Don's Jaguar XJ. A generous man, Don wanted to reward us with cash for serving him and his company. I told him we were not allowed to receive cash outside of our salary and certain allowances. We were working with what is now CRU International, which had a specific organizational and financial structure. But I did tell Don there was a $2,000 plumbing bill for a new sewer line at our house in Atlanta that I was having trouble paying. He asked me to send him the bill. A blessing! This off-site workshop was a great experience for all of us.

I was able to serve this man and his business. I enjoyed the preparation, the teaching, and the facilitating role I played. Suzanne gave me high marks too! I shared biblical teachings made practical, and I saw immediate improvement in the lives of these good brothers and sisters in Christ.

God used this whole experience to start me thinking. Was there any way I could do this type of work going forward? My wheels were turning.

The answer was a not-for-profit Christian ministry working in partnership with a for-profit business. I did not want to be serving men only with Bible verses and biblical counsel. I intended to show them how to live in their marriages, their families, and their businesses. This would be done with professional consultation, and they would pay fees. They would not take us seriously if they did not pay for our services.

Suzanne was inclined to be very anxious about the whole matter. We had left Philadelphia because we could not survive in that performance environment, and now the leadership of the organization was shifting back to Philadelphia. This spooked Suzanne, and she didn't scare easily. She put some pressure on me, saying, "Chris, you have to get us out of here."

When I told Colonel Mac what I was facing at home, he advised, "Chris, buy some time!" It was solidly good advice coming from an older man who had seen his share of corporate politics and disappointments. Pain.

This was not a time for any kind of haste. There was no need to jump ship. We would have some time for some strategic planning. I told Suzanne, "Cool it. If we leave Executive Ministries, it will be when God opens the door." Suzanne spent more time with the Lord.

So now I had the vision and the organizational strategy. It was time for action. We even had our first product, the Management Productivity Workshop.

CHAPTER 24

Josh

Around 1986, ten years after her new birth in Christ, Suzanne began to develop a heart for children in hard places. From finding child-raising difficult, over the last ten years she had become a supermom, making sure that the needs of her children, Christopher, now fourteen, and Colin, twelve, were met. Nothing would get in the way of that objective.

But now, apparently, she was being prepared for another assignment involving children. She watched a documentary on orphans in Guatemala and wept. "Chris, is the Lord calling me to start an orphanage?" She had the talent to do so. The Lord was giving her a burden, much the way he had given me a vision for male spiritual leadership.

Nehemiah's story in the Bible reminds us that whenever God uses a person to accomplish his work, it all begins with a burden. In his 1958 book *Victorious Christian Service,* Alan Redpath put it this way: "Nehemiah was called to build the wall around Jerusalem that the Babylonians had torn down, but first he had to weep over the ruins."

It turned out that Suzanne's assignment was not to build an orphanage. It would not involve stones or bricks or mortar at all. It would involve a two-year-old boy in our own family.

In October 1987, Suzanne and I traveled to Connecticut to attend the wedding of my brother Eddie and his fiancée, Carol. After the wedding, we were at my mother's house in Waterbury, and my sister Leslie, eighteen years younger than I, asked if I would look at her car that was stranded in front of the house, refusing to start.

As though it was yesterday, I remember the passenger car door opening and a cute toddler jumping up on the seat and exclaiming, "Come on, Uncle Chris, let's go for a ride." His name was Joshua. I was somewhat taken with him, but neither Suzanne nor I thought much more about him when we returned to Atlanta.

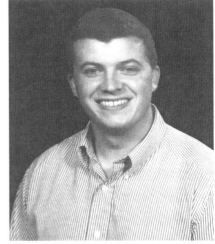

A month later I called my parents in Connecticut for a Thanksgiving Day chat, and during our conversation, my mother told me that she and my father were tasked with taking care of Joshua. My sister Marybeth told me Josh was now under the custody of the probate court in Waterbury.

He was the second child that Leslie had brought into the world and would not raise. Marybeth had taken care of Josh's sister, Katie, for some time. There would be a third

My son Josh.

child later. What a heartbreaking situation. Little Josh was being passed from one home to the next, even to neighbors, in an attempt to take care of him.

The family was stressed. My father, who was suffering from post-occupational depression, did nothing more than sit in a chair, and when he saw his state-appointed psychiatrist, he lamented over the loss of his bus! My mother said that the psychiatrist exclaimed to my father, "Whitey, if you don't stop talking about that @#$& bus! You are driving me crazy." My mother told me about this, trying to keep a sense of humor amid all the strain.

The talk with my mother left me heavy-hearted. Later that Thanksgiving morning, while I was shaving, Suzanne banged on the bathroom door. "What is going on with your family?" she wanted to know.

"You will never believe it," I said. "My parents have got Joshua." There was silence.

Suzanne came back not too long later, and with that same unmistakable clarity as when she'd told me about asking Christ to come into her life ten years earlier, she declared, "We need to take that boy!"

I don't know where my words of wisdom came from, but I blurted out, "You had better make the phone call, because my life will not change that much. But yours certainly will."

Two days later, on Saturday morning, a Delta jet pulled up to the gate, and off came Josh with his aunt Marybeth. She stayed a few days to ensure a safe transition, and Joshua never left our home in Atlanta for the rest of his childhood.

Before Marybeth returned home, I overheard Joshua tell her, "You know, Auntie Mary, this is a very nice house." This vulnerable little boy's awareness of his physical security at that young age made a deep impression on my soul.

I traveled to Connecticut to visit with a judge a few times before he gave us custody. With my lawyer at my side, Judge Lawlor said sternly, "Mr. White, most of the children who come through this court have no chance. With you and your family, he might have a chance." The lawyer said that he had never seen the judge act so quickly on a matter.

Christopher and Colin now had a little brother to pour their lives into. Christopher remembered: "One of the first things I can think about was taking Josh trick-or-treating. He loved going out, and Colin and I were proud brothers to take him through the neighborhood.

Left to right: Josh with Pat Reynolds ("Miss Pat") and Miriam Heiskell at school; Josh and I enjoying a day on the beach.

123

Mom made him a pirate outfit, and Josh made funny, almost karate-like moves in his pirate costume."

Colin, a natural teacher, took Josh under his wing. When Colin was older and at Marine Officer Candidates School in Quantico, Virginia, we all piled into the family Chevy station wagon, with Christopher driving, and went to his graduation. Seeing two hundred marine officer candidates drilling on the tarmac in perfect unison, rifle butts hitting the deck with a crack, greatly touched Josh. For the next two weeks he lived and slept in a pair of rolled-up fatigues.

Christopher, Colin and Josh White

When Colin's West Coast tour of duty was over and he was preparing to transfer to Fort Benning, Georgia, to work as liaison with the army, he flew Josh to California. The older brother and the little brother meandered across the country on the way home.

Suzanne, of course, felt the weight more than all of us. She was in her late forties with two teenagers who were starting to become less dependent. We could even go out for a couple of hours on occasion without having to hunt down a babysitter. But now, the age meter was dialed back to two. One morning, very early, I woke up to see Suzanne sitting up in bed and sobbing. "I can't do this. My whole life is turned upside down."

I panicked and called a friend who was a clinical psychologist. Chuck Carr was true to form. With totally calm objectivity, he said, "Chris, you and Suzanne do not have an organic problem, you have a management problem." Suzanne was emboldened by that challenge, and we managed through all of this together. Josh's arrival in our family is a wonderful memory for all of us.

———————

When Josh was two,
before we could get custody,
a judge asked me to send him
a letter articulating what I saw as
the risk and what commitment
I, principally, and my family
would be willing to make.
By God's grace, thirty-four
years later we are hanging
in there together. All of us.
God has given us grace.

———————

Nine years later, when Josh was eleven, we were able to officially adopt him into our family. It took nine years because there was no cooperation on the part of Joshua's birth parents. His father, who had abandoned the family when Josh was three months old, would not even acknowledge receipt of notification of the hearing. But a good Atlanta custody attorney powered us through, and the judge ruled on abandonment.

When Josh was two, before we could get custody, a judge asked me to send him a letter articulating what I saw as the risk and what commitment I, principally, and my family would be willing to make. By God's grace, thirty-five years later we are hanging in there together. All of us. God has given us grace.

Left: Josh White and son Jeremiah; Right: Josh, wife Nicole and son Daniel.

Mark Christopher

In the early 1990s, Mark Christopher called me. He was a top real estate broker in Atlanta, and he was actively involved in reaching out to men in his sphere. As a total self-starter he had assembled a small men's group who met regularly. When Mark and I first met for lunch, we saw eye to eye. He asked if we would allow him to bring his group to our growing FMMF. Mark had visited a couple of times, and he saw the advantage of having several tables of men meeting together in one place. Our team had also built a strong logistical support. When he agreed to take basic training, according to our best practices, we gave him the green light. Mark became a valuable member of our leadership team. He quickly became part of our monthly First Cut Leadership Forum. Mark became a good friend and eventually joined our advisory board. He was what we call a FAT man (faithful, available and teachable). He was always hospitable.

Mark Christopher

Mark and his wife, Nancy, invited Suzanne and me to dinner. While we regularly hosted couples in our home, it was a great treat to be invited out. Hospitality, what the Bible calls a "love of strangers" (Romans 12:13; Hebrews 13:2) is a lost art for many today in our increasingly diverse society.

That night with Mark and Nancy, Mark was strikingly dressed in white duck trousers with red suspenders. After dinner, I saw him in front of the fireplace and noticed what a handsome man he was. I even asked myself, "I wonder what God is going to do with this man. What has God planned for this man in full." This blond, blue-eyed professional made a lot of money, and he and his attractive, sophisticated wife possessed the Southern skills necessary for success. He was a great golfer and fisherman, and he was comfortable with shotguns. What was God's plan for his life?

One day I told Mark I was on my way to meet Snyder Turner, a lawyer and the pastor of Calvary Children's Home. Snyder was counseling me regarding my options as our son Joshua was bonding with our family. We did not yet have permanent legal custody, and the situation made me very nervous. What a wonderful thing to be able to talk to a man who had been part of scores of custodial matters, who loved the Lord, and who knew the law. Mark asked if he could come along. Long story short, that connection resulted in Mark and Nancy adopting two small children through Snyder: Coleman and Laura Logan. Those children, like my precious Joshua, found a loving home despite a hard start. So of course this common experience for our families also helped to increase our friendship.

In the late 1990s, Mark's father, Chris, called me from St. Joseph's Hospital and asked me to come over. Mark had just gone through diagnostic surgery for an abnormality in his chest. The diagnosis was adenocarcinoma, a cancer in the chest cavity lining. His prognosis was six months. Of course, Mark and Nancy and their good friend and nurse Ellen LaGrone put up a good fight: chemo, diet, and most of all prayer. Mark's boss,

127

Mike Elting, set up a prayer hotline for people to call in with their prayers and support. Each week Mark left a message on the hotline with an update on his condition and his own words of inspiration, challenge, and encouragement. He often repeated the refrain, "Don't think you have more time. Look at me. Good health. Never smoked. And I am dying at forty-three years of age. Don't assume you have more time, be reconciled to God." Mark and his team stretched the six-month prognosis to eighteen months.

Mark and Nancy gave me the privilege of bringing the message at Mark's funeral at a local megachurch. I used the imagery of a diamond in my eulogy. Diamonds are formed when carbon deposits

A large-scale prayer breakfast is still held annually in Mark Christopher's honor.

deep within the earth are subjected to high temperatures and enormous pressures. As the pressure of Mark's pain and the debilitating chemotherapy increased, his witness and preaching became bolder and brighter. In his last hotline message just days before his death, Mark repeated his message to his friends. Despite frequent coughing, he got through it and again concluded his message with "Don't think you have more time. Be reconciled to God."

The Atlanta real estate community had scheduled Mark to speak at a prayer breakfast being held in his honor. Mark died prior to the event. Instead, the program that morning was delivered through several testimonies from men whose lives had been touched by Mark. Steve Cesari was one of them. I met him at Mark's gravesite. Steve became part of our fellowship and joined the First Cut Leadership Forum. Later, he went on to start Iron Man, an adaptation of the FMMF concept. That ministry continues today.

For the last twenty-one years—including two years lost to the pandemic—the annual real estate prayer breakfast in honor of Mark Christopher has been held at the Cobb Galleria Conference Center. Attendance averaged five hundred in the beginning. It was capped

———

Don't think you have
more time. Look at me.
Good health. Never smoked.
And I am dying at forty-three
years of age. Don't assume
you have more time,
be reconciled to God.

MARK CHRISTOPHER

———

at twelve hundred and has been that way every year as long as I can remember. Hundreds of people have come to know the Lord through the annual prayer breakfast. Many more have rededicated their lives or used the breakfast to connect as a fellowship group.

Over the years, through the Mark Christopher program, we have been able to help men in transition: divorce, job loss, an inability to pay bills, career counseling. We do whatever we can through a fund set up for benevolent giving after Mark's death.

Mark Christopher is another example of what can happen when one man reaches out to another with the love of Jesus Christ.

CHAPTER 25

Leadership Companies Start-Up

Now, on the mission front in the fall of 1986, it was time for action. I met with the new leader of Executive Ministries, Dave Balch, in Atlanta. He had been my mentor in Philadelphia before we left in 1980. He was accompanied by Steve Douglas, the heir apparent to Bill Bright. I told them my vision for ministry had moved to a long-term focus on the men in Atlanta. I wanted to develop this work myself.

My vision was to see every man take his rightful, God-given responsibility seriously and find his calling. That is what God had done for me. We men need to integrate our faith into our primary institutions: marriage, family, and business. Both Steve and Dave were cooperative.

After reading Os Guinness's 1993 book, *The American Hour,* I took the last $250 in our checking account and flew to Washington, DC, to talk with Os personally. He took me to his library and gave me everything he had on the whole concept of "calling." Helping men to find their calling was what I wanted to do. And I planned to do this through patient, long-term relationships with men, helping them to see that God had made each of them for a purpose. No one else can better do what God has called them to do.

This was the vision that drove our new primitively small organization dedicated to leadership development. This new organization, Leadership Ministries Inc. (LMI), would have a companion consultancy, the Leadership Development Company (LDC). Now, it needed some fuel—a little capital—and all kinds of organizational and administrative muscle. The start-up was strenuous, but the freedom offered by this new organization was more valuable to Suzanne and me. Risk was not a dissuader but rather a motivator to us because it was accompanied by freedom.

Bill Carter, an attorney and a new follower of Jesus Christ, guided our application to the IRS for tax-exempt status. Initially, two benefactors helped financially—Jim Bell, who, with his wife, Ida, hosted several outreach dinner parties, and Don Hughes, the Memphis entrepreneur.

The Friday Morning Men's Fellowship, which I was leading, continued to grow. Every week I met with men personally at a Houlihan's restaurant. I brought the message three times a month. On the fourth Friday, other men shared their testimony.

Much of the business consulting was informal and initially pro bono, but by God's grace, Don Hughes was gaining momentum with his business, and he asked for my help. For the next eighteen months I flew to Memphis every Sunday night, stayed with Don and Marcia, and gave him a full day's work before returning to Atlanta on Tuesday. My biggest contribution was to help him practice the skills we had taught him at the off-site retreat months earlier.

So much credit goes to Don. In his business he was the financial genius and chief salesman around whom everything depended. Thinking he could leverage himself with more salesmen, he was loading up with overhead. For a while his top-line revenue was so strong he was almost getting away with it. But the price he was paying was frustration. He could not understand why the other people could not do things the way he did. Don had the temperament, the expertise, and, frankly, the charm and confidence needed to convince a scared S&L executive he could help him. Not everyone could do this.

Jim Bell, a real estate developer, was trying to get a new property, Perimeter 400, off the ground in a tough, competitive economy, and he needed tenants and cars in the parking lot to show momentum. He gave us eighty square feet of windowless interior office space with free rent.

I came into the office for part of the day and then spent the rest of the day out with men. Suzanne came in a few hours a week. One day I might be helping a man with the assurance of his salvation and getting him started on a program for daily time with God, and another afternoon I might be helping a man think through his approach to resolving a conflict he was having with an unproductive employee. I was thoroughly enjoying the freedoms this bi-vocational model gave me. Ninety-five percent of the people who had been donating money to our ministry stayed with us. They liked our vision.

The worst decisions I made going forward were in trying to cut corners and accelerate the growth of the Leadership companies in my time. Realistically, the best training for effective consulting is to consult on the job. If I had known then what I know now, I could have been much more helpful to Don. Consultants learn at the expense of their early clients.

Administration is real. If you do not have good financial and administrative support, it will cripple an embryonic ministry such as ours. We sent Suzanne to the Johnson O'Connor Research Foundation to have her aptitudes tested. How could she be utilized most promisingly to help this work?

The testing showed objectively why she had been so effective in the retail fashion industry in New York. Suzanne had a natural ability to chew

From left: Carl Brigham, Dick McCormick, Toney Pozek, myself and Suzanne.

—————

"Howard, all I can tell you is
that I feel very alone," I said.
"Who is your bridge?"
he asked quietly.
I got a little defensive.
"What do you mean, Howard?"
"Chris, is Jesus your bridge?
Then, walk over that bridge."

—————

up paperwork, manage finances, and problem-solve creatively. She had a mind like a steel trap.

I thanked God our values were in sync, because otherwise we would have ended up stressing each other out. She had a "quick" personality, and I am "inefficient" by nature. I sometimes stewed over things for hours, even days, before going into action. Pace was our biggest stress point. Over the last fifty years, we learned how to put less stress on each other. It was good work.

I would get feelings of anxiety when I found myself professionally alone. For the previous eighteen years, I had been in corporate systems. There was always someone to talk with, someone to bounce ideas off. Sometimes sitting alone in our eighty-square foot office, I began to feel uneasy and panicky.

One week I flew to Philadelphia to see our old friends and investors and bring them up to date. I called Howard Blandau, the professional counselor who had helped Suzanne and me integrate our new Christian faith into our marriage and work years earlier. He agreed to meet me for dinner on a Saturday night at a restaurant.

We sat in a booth out of the way. Howard went right at it. "Chris, what kind of feelings are you having?"

"Howard, all I can tell you is that I feel very alone," I said.

"Who is your bridge?" he asked quietly.

I got a little defensive. "What do you mean, Howard?"

"Chris, is Jesus your bridge? Then, walk over that bridge."

Amazingly, in a two-hour dinner meeting with a gifted man of God, I regained my footing and returned to Atlanta more confident. I still thank Howard effusively for being so helpful to Suzanne and me.

We made the Friday Morning Men's Fellowship our official flagship product. There, Suzanne and I found a healthy partnership in message preparation. I might spend ten to fifteen hours preparing for a fifteen-minute message (an hour per minute). I learned never to give a new message without running it by Suzanne. She would listen and then, like a skilled surgeon with a scalpel, cut out and rearrange the material. Suzanne was "bone of my bone" and the other side of my brain.

Chuck Honess, entrepreneur, business consultant, and Leadership Ministries advisory board member, gave Suzanne all the manual record keeping and accounting tools we would need. Now, we had an administrator-plus who was "free overhead." This is one of the tricks of small company start-ups, and Suzanne was a natural. From that point forward, I never saw a check, a tax form, or any accounting. She did it all until years later, when we could bump the overhead with more support.

———————————————

My vision was to see
every man take his rightful,
God-given responsibility
seriously and lead by developing a
personal vision to take
creative control of his life and
find his calling. That is what
God had done for me.
We men need to integrate
our faith into our primary
institutions: marriage, family,
and business.

———————————————

CHAPTER 26

Gaining Momentum

The Friday Morning Men's Fellowship continued to grow at a strong pace, which added to the pressures. The logistics included keeping track of registration cards and, from the start of the ministry, the token dollar-a-week we charged the men for their doughnuts, orange juice, and coffee. Donor communication is key, and Suzanne wrote personal notes to each investor every time they sent a check.

It is important to reiterate here that the FMMF has been effective in large measure because it is indeed a neutral ground for those who attend. They realize no demands are placed on them, no dues need to be paid, and no membership is required. It is a beautiful concept that works. This gives a man the time he needs to come to faith, to grow, and to become part of, even give his life to, the work of Christ. Again, we have always appreciated the people who modeled this for us. Art and Nancy DeMoss and Dave and Dianne Balch.

For our new work, none of this could have happened without our angel investors: Jim Bell, Don Hughes, and others who became involved.

During this stressful transition time, I was swimming for exercise during the lunch hour at a church health club not too far from the office. Several times an older man was there at the same time, except he walked around the track over the pool. I introduced myself to him in the locker room. He was Carl Brigham.

We chatted for a while, and I had my evangelist hat on. We agreed to meet for lunch to get better acquainted. Over lunch I learned Carl had been a certified management consultant for thirty years and had a wealth of experience. Five years earlier he had been misdiagnosed with a heart condition that turned out to be an aneurysm, which was corrected surgically. But in the process he had lost all momentum with his consulting practice.

Probing further, which is my way, I discovered he was a Christian Scientist. They follow the teachings of Mary Baker Eddy, which are not biblically orthodox, but practitioners are good thinkers. They are "scientists."

Carl was seventy years old when I met him. He and his wife, Marilyn, were largely dependent on their Social Security income at that time, but he had a little more professional gas left in his tank, and I was desperate for someone to talk to at the office. I needed a sounding board.

We hired Carl at three hundred dollars a month to be with me and help build our Leadership Companies. Meanwhile, Jim Bell gave us another eighty square feet of space.

I never tried to talk Carl out of his Christian Science faith, but I did bring him and Marilyn to a dinner sponsored by our host couples at which Chuck Colson of Watergate fame was the speaker.

Carl Brigham, the "watchdog"

Bingo! As soon as Carl heard the gospel of Jesus Christ, he received the Lord and was converted. There was no equivocation. This dear man experienced the grace of Jesus Christ at age seventy, which is rare, but God's provision is unique, custom-made for each person's needs.

Could it be, might our sovereign, merciful God have waited to call Carl Brigham to himself "for such a time as this" (Esther 4:14)? God knew when Carl was ready, and God tells us He will "meet all [our] needs according to the riches of His glory in Christ Jesus" (Philippians 4:19).

Carl, too, was an answer to my prayers. He became a new disciple in the faith and a wise counselor, a sounding board, to help me maneuver through myriad issues. Revenue challenges, for instance, haunted us. For years, just making payroll was tough. Putting younger Christians on the board, which we did despite attorney Terry Parker's advice not to do so, proved to be unwise. Some were uncomfortable in the role of advisor at their early stage of spiritual maturity. Carl, however, phrased his role a little differently. He said he played the role of "watchdog."

We plugged Marilyn Brigham into a Christian women's Bible study, and it did not go well. Well-meaning women bombarded her with literature that defined Christian Science as a cult. That is a word I never use with men. Carl was irritated by this attack on Marilyn, but he only said, "We were in error," with a tone of "no more, that's enough." He had an impressive air of authority.

Looking back, we were too fragile. We should have failed. But I was getting energy, particularly from seeing Carl grow like a weed. A relative gave Carl a week at the beach, and he asked me for a study assignment to take on his beach trip. Can you imagine? His humility in Christ energized me. I told him I wanted him to outline the book of Romans, and I taught him how to do that by using a book chart.

I had learned the technique in grad school. He got all over this spiritual exercise and came back with some real spiritual muscle. He developed confidence! In all my years of doing this work, I have never seen a man so hungry, "as newborn babes, desire the sincere milk of the word, that ye may grow thereby" (1 Peter 2:2 KJV). What a beautiful experience. A seventy-year-old baby Christian. For five years Carl gave me everything he had.

For a year or so our team consisted of Suzanne and me and Carl the watchdog. He more than paid for himself, especially with wisdom born from the school of hard knocks. Carl said, "Chris, I have made all of the mistakes. There is no need for us to have to make them all over again."

Bob Day, who was managing Edwards-Day Real Estate, hired Carl to help him think through his business strategy. Carl helped Bob to realize his real clients were the brokers who worked for him. Motivated brokers are happy brokers, and happy brokers are more productive. Increased market share follows. Carl made his clients work at thinking; that was his strength. Bob called him "the glacier," because Carl kept coming at him, slowly and thoroughly.

One day Carl scolded me. "Chris, you are doing too much thinking for the client." Over time, I became less player-coach and more a mentor who keeps men thinking straight.

I treat all the men I serve as clients, whether they donated money to Leadership Ministries Inc. (LMI) or paid consulting fees for Leadership Development Company (LDC). I served them all professionally. I earned their trust through loving professionalism.

Eventually, LDC ended up with four basic professional service offerings, and all of them were built around our experiences with strategic life choices. They were:

Life and Career Planning, which is one-on-one, face-to-face interaction to develop a life and career plan within a relationship of trust. This is our flagship product. It applies to people of all ages, from teens anticipating college to people anticipating retirement.

Executive Communication, which addresses the number-one problem in American business today through our three-point approach: relate, communicate, and resolve conflict.

Strategic Business Thinking and Planning, which helps clients think and talk through difficult issues with their team, develop their people, or, when needed, to dismiss some.

Personnel Selection, which helps clients find the right person for a position. We have found a person's track record is the strongest indicator of future results.

Toney Pozek

All of these products have a slant toward the soft side—the people-relational side versus the hard side of finance and logistics—to perfectly complement the nonprofit work of the Friday Morning Men's Fellowship.

We eventually got enough steam in the boiler and started looking for some administrative support. I met Toney Pozek, a mother at our boys' school, Mount Vernon Christian Academy, and she was looking for part-time work. Carl said we needed a girl Friday, showing how dated he was. He said, "We need a doormat." Yikes! We got more than we bargained for with Toney—and she was no doormat!

Toney was a resourceful administrator, and she and Carl developed a considerable tension that's unavoidable when two creative personalities vie to control an organization's priorities. Yet that tension allowed us to accomplish a great deal. Carl was forced to treat Toney as a teammate. He did not like that, but he still had a lot to learn. He was young in Christ, though he was growing fast.

At about the same time, Joe Hope, a successful insurance broker and financial planner, wanted to spin out of the Houlihan's FMMF with a separate group of men. Carl came alongside Joe to help him. True to form, Carl became a trusted advisor to Joe, and the small group they founded met at Colony Square in midtown Atlanta.

Joe Hope

One of Joe's clients hired Carl to consult when she launched a medical services organization. Carl served there a year. One day she called me and said that Carl was falling asleep in her office. She diagnosed him quickly and correctly: he was starting to shut down. Years of hard living were catching up with him. Not much later, he suffered a stroke.

When I visited him at the hospital, he expressed concern about not being at the office. God gave me the grace to say, "Carl, don't worry. You will always have a place at Leadership Development Company." Sadly, he never left the hospital.

Carl's funeral at Patterson's Oglethorpe Hill Chapel was conducted by a Christian Science practitioner who was very amiable and positive when I told her that several men Carl had worked with wanted to share a word of testimony. They spoke of how Carl's counsel had been wise and practical, and there was just enough "salt of the gospel" in their testimonies to be appropriate.

We wanted to honor Carl and follow God's guidance to "Be wise in the way you act toward outsiders… Let your conversation be always full of

141

grace, seasoned with salt, so that you may know how to answer everyone" (Colossians 4:5–6). I was proud of our men for their sense of decorum. Carl Brigham is another testimony of special grace and provision for our struggling gospel ministry. Look for Carl in heaven.

Bill Carter gave us a Tandy computer with ten megabytes of mainframe memory. That computer was so small, compared to later ones, it would be hard to describe. Mega means millions. Today, we use terabytes—millions of megas—to measure computer data storage capabilities.

Jerry West, a FMMF man and a computer contractor and college professor, put every byte of that computer to work for us. He installed the very first PC relational database management tool ever: R Base. I designed the basic documents we would need to run the companies effectively, and Jerry and our administrator, Toney, took it from there.

Even today, thirty years later, Jerry serves LDC as a volunteer. He has always been a good friend. When he saw I was under a lot of pressure and pretty much always in a survival mode, he cared enough about me to put me on his fitness program. He came to my house, put up a laminated wall calendar, and gave me a grease pencil to keep track of my exercise and see starkly how many days I was working out. I faithfully used my NordicTrack three times a week until arthritis finally overtook me. Now I am on the NuStep machine, and I have a Medtronic spinal cord stimulator implant that keeps me in the game.

Jerry is supportive of the ministry and a constant source of encouragement. He is another strategic provision of God for the mission of LDC. His testimony is evidence of how God's grace was working in the lives of men here in Atlanta.

CHAPTER 27

Growth and Expansion

Mike Taylor had spun out of Houlihan's FMMF with a group of
men to the Chequers Restaurant near the Perimeter Mall. During the recession of the 1980s,
Mike brought a job search, networking angle to
the FMMF. The needs of unemployed men in
Atlanta were so acute that for a while we had
about 150 men filling Chequers every Friday
morning.

Among the men who joined that group was
Charlie Paparelli, an investor and business powerhouse who later went on to head a ministry to the

Mike Taylor

technology business community. In a post on his blog awhile back, Charlie
described his first encounter with the FMMF:

> At 7:00 a.m. I walked through the front doors of the restaurant. I was
> greeted by a man my age… [He said,] "Welcome to the Friday Morning
> Men's Fellowship. Is this your first time?"
>
> He had me fill out a name tag and then pointed me to the coffee and
> doughnut bar laid out for the guests. It was a friendly crowd. A couple of
> men introduced themselves, but I was more interested in keeping a low profile.
>
> After all, I had no idea how to conduct myself in a Christian fellowship.
> I didn't know what to expect. Would they call on me to speak? Ask me to read

*the Bible or, worse yet, tell them why I had come in the first place? What
was I going to say? "I'm looking for my higher power? Have you seen him?"*

Charlie told how he listened to a scripture reading and then a short
talk by the speaker (it happened to be me). Afterward, he was directed
to a table where he met five other men. "The leader asked for prayer requests," Charlie recalled. "Each man gave an update of what was going
on in his life. I was struck by how transparent these men were about their
lives, families, and business challenges. Some of the stories were pretty
horrible. Parents with cancer, wayward kids, marriages not working, no
job or income, bad bosses, and the list went on. I was thinking, 'I'm in
AA and can't seem to figure out what I'm going to do professionally, but
my wife and kids love me. I'm in pretty good shape.' But I didn't share
any of this. I was there to observe and learn."

During the discussion that followed, Charlie grew more comfortable.
"These guys are just like me. They are struggling with life and searching
for answers. They're here because they believe God has the answers. They
think the answers to their questions can be found in the Bible, I thought
to myself," he wrote.

"At the end of our time together, each of the men thanked me for
coming and asked me to join them the next week. I liked these guys. They
were not like the people I was meeting while networking in the community. They were authentic and transparent, unguarded. I wanted to be
authentic and transparent. Maybe this was a place I could be that way."
(To read the rest of Charlie's blog post, see Chapter 34.)

Dick McCormick had developed a small business consulting practice
with an emphasis on good financial management. He worked with us as a
consultant. We still use today many of the tools he developed to help men
get their arms around their money issues.

Countless times I have seen major stress reductions with men and
their marriages simply by helping them with a net worth statement and
a simple budgeting plan. This is another biblical truth: "Any enterprise
is built by wise planning, becomes strong through common sense, and
profits wonderfully by keeping abreast of the facts" (Proverbs 24:3-4
TLB). I am convinced that if a man learns the basics of marriage and
money, the "M&M's" so to speak, he will have solved many of his
problems.

Marriage involves learning the art of loving your wife by meeting her needs. Love her in an understanding and unconditional way. Husbands, in the same way, you and your wife are trusting the "Shepherd and Overseer of [our] souls" (1 Peter 2:25), Jesus Christ. "Be considerate as you live with your wives, and treat them with respect as the weaker partner and as heirs with you of the gracious gift of life, so that nothing will hinder your prayers" (1 Peter 3:7-8). Peter is telling us to "be creative." Think about her unique makeup. Help her to be the woman and the wife God wants her to be. That is a full-time job. The rewards are a partner who will meet your needs and help you to be a more productive and loving husband. You are companions, partners, collaborators.

Money involves keen financial planning, as Tom Stanley's model from his 1996 book, *The Millionaire Next Door,* illustrates. I was Tom's Sunday school teacher for a year. His advice is extremely simple:

1. Do work that you are good at. Find your calling!
2. Spend less than you make.
3. Invest the difference aggressively to build wealth.

When Mike Taylor moved on from the Chequers group, Dick McCormick took over as the group leader. Today, the restaurant is no longer at the Perimeter location. That prize piece of real estate near the MARTA station became the formidable-looking regional headquarters for State Farm Insurance. Our Perimeter ministry subsequently moved to Tin Lizzy's Cantina when Chequers closed.

Matt Lacey had a strong background in ministry development, and he joined our staff and fit right into our bi-vocational model. He

Matt and Katy Lacey

brought a special caring and compassionate dimension to the leadership position at our Perimeter location. He went on to earn a seminary degree and become a hospital chaplain. Matt goes where people are hurting. That is his special gift.

The best contract Matt ever engineered at LDC is the one he made with Katy Ellis, our business manager. They were married on May 24, 2014. Matt and Katy now enjoy serving people together.

Dan Gardner had been a youth pastor before he joined our staff and gave us four very productive years. He was one of the most talented men I ever worked with anywhere.

CHAPTER 28

The Missing Link

In his 2001 book, *Good to Great*, Jim Collins describes the flywheel effect. A flywheel keeps an automobile engine spinning between power strokes. The flywheel is huge, heavy, and creaky. It takes a lot of effort to move it, but you keep pushing and pushing. And then, when it gets going, it provides momentum because it is hard to stop.

Leadership Ministries Inc. was hard to get going, but we were gaining momentum. We had a great, solid concept in that it is built around meeting the needs of men.

We create environments where men experience real fellowship, which is a missing link in so many men's lives. This has been true with all our products. Our Life and Career Planning process is primarily one-on-one, which is a special, intense fellowship. We meet with clients weekly and create a safe place where they can really think about their life and career.

The flywheel was rolling in the FMMF. We were

Suzanne, Howard Hendricks and me

developing new table leaders monthly, which is critical because they are the backbone of the ministry. This is one of my favorite activities, training table leaders: giving a man the simple tools to facilitate meaningful discussion with the men at his table around the Word of God.

I built a model of a typical table discussion from the work of Howard Hendricks, the gold standard in leadership training. His work on leadership has been foundational to me and my work. We teach table leaders that every meeting should have the following elements:

• **Personalization:** A question is shared that gives each man a chance to share himself. "What was your favorite job?" "Tell us about the best boss you have ever had?" "How was discipline administered in your family when you were growing up?" These questions lead into the biblical topic of the day.

• **Polarization:** Good polarity means good discussion around the Word of God. Table leaders ask good questions after they learn to begin questions with who, what, why, when, where, or how. "What do you see in that paragraph and how might that apply to you?" Good discussion helps men to discover truth. This discipline is called discovery Bible study. The key is involvement, which is another critical ingredient to the FMMF's success.

• **Purpose Realization:** Each week table leaders make sure the men realize the purpose planned for that session. It is okay to drive the message home. Preach a little. Emphasize what the men need to learn. By asking good questions and listening, you have earned the right to be heard. The table leader's mission is to ensure the men receive strong biblical truths centered around a cohesive biblical purpose. We coach our table leaders to act like chairmen and lead good discussions around God's Word.

These three principles make up our 3P model. We taught this model at a monthly meeting we call the First Cut Leadership Forum for our table leaders. This is a place where we take more time than we do on Friday mornings. Leaders communicate with symbols. So we met on the first Monday of every month at 6:30 a.m. for an hour and a half. We give the Lord's work the "first cut." Jeff Shaw, now a board member, joined the leadership team about this time. Many of these men—Jim Gray, Steve O'Day, Ralph Rowland, Earl Young, David Dorries, Bob Day, Bob Voyles, Steve Weidman, Doug Chrietzberg, Jeff Muir, Tom Wesley, and

Post-pandemic, some of our Friday table groups meet in a hybrid format, with some in-person and others online.

Christopher White—are still leading tables in person, remotely by Zoom, or a combination of the two.

The concept of giving the Lord the first cut was another gift to me from Arthur DeMoss, who said, "Our Lord wants the first cut of everything: time, talent, treasure, schedules, and habits."

I am amazed at how receptive men have been to the challenge of studying books like *The Training of the Twelve* by Dr. A. B. Bruce. This book was written over 150 years ago (1871) by this Scottish scholar and exegete. Our friend Dr. John Musselman, founder of the Jackson Institute, modernized the language without losing any of its impact. We took four years to study that incredible book, which Howard Hendricks called the finest work of exegesis ever.

The Reformed Pastor, written circa 1660, was modernized by Dr. James Houston, founder of Regent College in Vancouver, British Columbia. It took us two years to study this classic. I took Dr. Houston's book and spent a week at the beach making it into a study tool with questions to be used to focus concentration. Men who live in this distracted culture need that kind of help.

Now, all that pushing of the flywheel was starting to pay off.

More men, across all kinds of demographic lines, were getting involved. Some were barbers and cooks and some had high-leverage careers in real estate, finance, and investments.

Ken Thrasher started coming to Friday mornings in 1986. He became part of our board and to this day has been a rock of integrity, a wise counsel, and a source of encouragement.

Jeff Muir, the founder of Fulcrum Equity Partners, which invests in rapidly growing companies that need capital to increase their momentum and profits, came to a meeting I called to talk about our finances. Jeff is a great listener, and after listening intently to all the free advice filling the room, he simply and quietly took out his checkbook and wrote a big check.

Jeff became a table leader, and before long he was recruiting men from his circle of influence. Several of these men were prominent and gave to the ministry proportionately. You can do things with money. Jeff helped increase the momentum.

Earl Young came off the bench during our teaching series on the letters to the seven churches in Revelation. To the church in Laodicea, Jesus said, "So, because you are lukewarm—neither hot nor cold—I am about to spit you out of my mouth" (Revelation 3:16). Earl made sure Jesus never had a reason to say anything like that to him. He has been a faithful table leader now for thirty-five years.

About this time Ralph Rowland started a table at the Chequers location, later moving to On the Border Mexican Grill and Cantina in Buckhead. He is still going. Almost simultaneously Larry Corbitt started to lead a table. These men are still going because they own their ministries and are called by God.

Jeff Muir　　　　　　　　　　　*Earl Young*

Left: Ken Thrasher; Right: Phil and Shirley Benton

I had been adamant, even bombastic, that our ministry would be different! I insisted we position the work quietly and keep a distinct environment. Critical to the success of this ministry was having tables as a unique place of relational refreshment for fellowship. It is what the Bible calls *koinonia*, communion through intimate participation. It is fragile and can slide backward into another religious meeting very easily. Media is no substitute for face-to-face personal interaction. Today, we use Zoom to accommodate men who can't attend in person. But the gospel is more incarnational than just informational.

Phil Benton ignored my edict and started secretly recording everything we did. Some of our best work is on our website, leadmin.org. (Look for The Ten Commandments, Ecclesiastes, Titus, Ruth, Nehemiah, Malachi, The Lord's Prayer, Hebrews 11, Jude, John 13–17, The Upper Room Discourse, and James.) Thank you, Phil.

My neighbor Jim had been talking about the FMMF with Doug Lyle, a colleague at the bank where they both worked. When Doug joined a Friday morning table, he became the next puzzle piece we needed in the development of the organization.

I was dedicated to mission, sales, preaching, teaching, and working with men. What I did not realize was how powerful good management could be for a leader like myself.

Doug had been a bank auditor before he retired, and we needed his special talents. He, like Suzanne, could walk into a messy situation and organize everything before he would walk out. It took Doug awhile to adjust to the fact that we were not a bank and much of what we do is unpredictable and serendipitous. But once he understood our culture, he was able to patiently organize us with a total finance, accounting, and management information system.

Doug positioned us for growth after many of the initial board members drifted off when their terms expired. We allowed the board to shrink to the minimum number that lawyer Terry Parker had suggested. But Doug encouraged David Butler, Carl Schwob, and me to hold down the fort. David and Carl were older and wiser, and I basked in their supportive fellowship.

Doug Lyle

One Saturday morning with Dave and Carl, I was venting about the pressure I was feeling. Dave said, "You can vent here but not out there." I had a safe place where I could confess my fears!

Eventually, we moved out of our free office space and became a client of Jim Bell in the same building, Perimeter 400 Center. I never thought we could do it, but one day we bit the overhead bullet and started to pay rent for about $2,000 per month. I knelt in my office late one afternoon and praised my faithful God.

The real advantage to having a first-class manager like Doug is that I would not have to fight the wrong battles. In any group activity such as ours, people flow in and out. The information was so good that the board and I could see these patterns clearly and conserve our energy for strategic meetings with investors. Then Doug encouraged me to add men to our board to increase the number of men who understood the issues and could thus help grow the ministry. I listened and insisted that, with few exceptions, board members be table leaders or mentors so that our meetings would be a fellowship of fellow shepherds.

It was indeed a privilege to be part of all this. Our board discussions centered on what was going on in men's lives. That was our business. With that understanding over the years, we grew the board to a dozen table leaders and mentors. We had, at one time, nine staff people serving as many as five hundred men meeting on Friday mornings. That's a lot of people working together—like heart, mind, and purpose.

Doug became a table leader and eventually would lead our efforts at Chequers and later at Tin Lizzy's. He gave us twenty years of faithful service on the staff. Even today, the systems he built for donor management are hanging tough.

For this writing project, Doug offered his insights on twenty-three years as a table leader. First, he said, since he was employed by LMI, he felt that being a table leader was part of his responsibilities. Second, he said, "It gave me a forum for influence." He added, "More recently, I stay involved because I came to love the men at my location."

The program's advantages in developing his leadership included "removal of a lot of baggage from my childhood and early adult life," Doug commented. "The Lord set me free from all that, as I learned that he didn't need my help with other people but wanted me to experience love in action toward those who I was able to help."

Thinking about what he enjoyed most in his role, he said, "I love the freedom to really be myself with the men. I am more authentic, and I can see the men know that." The biggest challenge "is letting other men step into my former roles. Letting this happen is strategic to the ongoing effectiveness

Doug and Latrelle Chrietzberg

of the FMMF, but figuring out what my new roles are is challenging."

People who invest in a ministry such as ours like to see good management. So if you are building something similar in scope to ours, keep pushing the flywheel until you get enough momentum to absorb good administrators and management overhead. You will not be sorry.

In terms of close, day-to-day support, for quite a few years I had the best of both worlds in two terrific women who worked closely with me.

When Latrelle Chrietzberg interviewed for a position with us, I asked her why she wanted to work for a comparatively "modest salary." She said, "Well, you do love people, don't you?"

With hyperbole I responded, "Let me tell you, I don't love people. I hate people, but God has commanded us to love them as if we liked them." She got my point and gave us eighteen great years.

Latrelle was our office receptionist and handled whatever else we needed her to do: editing tapes, typing client proposals, managing data, and reproducing manuals. Whatever Latrelle does, she does carefully and she does it right. When faced with a new project, she panics and then courageously stays with it until she gains confidence. And then she adds value, lots of value, perfection!

One morning, when I drafted a proposal for a prospective client, I told Latrelle I needed it for a lunch meeting, and I would be leaving at 11:45 a.m. At 11:40, I was standing at her desk and pleading with her to give it to me so I would be on time for my meeting. She would not hand it to me because it was not perfect. Finally, close to tears, I said, "Give me that proposal. Any proposal is better than no proposal."

Karen Smith Hall

At another time Latrelle saved me from myself when I made a relational error with Dr. Armand Hendee, a prominent retired ob-gyn surgeon and former head of Emory Hospital training. I had come on too strong with Dr. Hendee, laying down the law regarding our guidelines for giving his testimony at the FMMF. I learned you just do not tell a man of Armand Hendee's caliber, a Southern professional gentleman, how to give a talk. He called and talked to Latrelle. Dear Latrelle spent an hour on the phone with him and smoothed everything over on my behalf.

I saw that transaction as another example of God's providence protecting this work. Offending this wonderful man would have been an unforgivable breach. God gave us mercy. Incidentally, Dr. Hendee's testimony is on our LMI website, and it is a superbly sincere and well-crafted story of God's amazing grace.

Latrelle and her husband, Doug, have been faithful friends to this work for more than twenty years. Latrelle and Suzanne had a close rela-

It was indeed a privilege
to be part of all this.
Our board discussions
centered on what was going
on in men's lives. That was
our business. With that
understanding over the years, we
grew the board to a dozen table
leaders and mentors.

tionship. When it became time to move the office location, Doug Chrietz-berg engineered the whole move, and it was seamless.

A few years later we hired Karen Smith Hall to assist Latrelle part time with the office administration. Karen and Latrelle became good friends and worked closely together for many years. Karen was the perfect complement to the team. Nothing scares Karen. She will try anything. She is bold and has never met a stranger. She added a very friendly dimension to our staff team and is a great VP of First Impressions. When new clients came to the office, Karen made sure they felt at home and at ease. For twenty years she was a steady, faithful member of the team.

Karen is quick, and I enjoyed the speed of her turnaround on projects. Recently she took all the teachings I had given at the FMMF on the book of Malachi and edited them for production as a podcast. This study is for men who need weight, ballast in their spiritual lives. This anchor needed by every man is, most appropriately, found in the last book of the Old Testament before it gives way to the New Testament and its revelation of the gospel of our Lord Jesus Christ.

I have always been impressed by the care Karen gave to her father, L. B. Smith, a World War II veteran, when he was starting to decline. She took him to the Veterans Administration and did anything she could to serve her father. Her loving care fit so well with our emphasis on strong family values at LMI and in keeping with the divine admonition, "Anyone who does not provide for their relatives, and especially for their own household, has denied the faith and is worse than an unbeliever" (1 Timothy 5:8).

For the last twenty years I have greatly enjoyed working with Karen, and I love and appreciate her. Karen also helped with the editing of this book. So, as you can see, the Lord in His grace gave us the organization we needed in order to be effective. The high-water mark for the number of people on the payroll before the Great Recession (2007–2009) was nine people. And we saw good growth by being faithful to our mission and by reaching out to men. Undergirding all of this, of course, was prayer.

Every week we met as a staff and prayed for each other and for all the people and various projects we needed the Lord to guide. Suzanne kept us on track with a staff prayer journal, and we could see the Lord answering our prayers. Her leadership as our prayer coordinator was foundational to our growth moving forward.

I had been adamant,
even bombastic, that our
ministry would be different!
I insisted we position the work
quietly and keep a distinct
environment. Critical to the
success of this ministry was
having tables as a unique place
of relational refreshment for
fellowship. It is what the
Bible calls *koinonia*,
communion through
intimate participation.

So, over several years, the Lord built a team that was very productive. We were making disciples of Jesus Christ. Men were integrating their faith into their marriages, families, and businesses. I must say here that it is all God's grace, but the most strategic reason for our success was the decision I made years earlier in a little cabin in Tiger, Georgia, when I knew I had God's permission. The resulting bi-vocational model freed me. Suzanne and I, with our choleric temperaments, were very motivated to work hard, give everything we had, and enjoy ourselves. We were like two draft horses yoked together and pulling a weight together.

"Enjoy life with your wife, whom you love, all the days of this meaningless life that God has given you under the sun... Whatever your hand finds to do, do it with all your might" (Ecclesiastes 9:9–10).

CHAPTER 29

Renewal of Christian Education

On a Wednesday afternoon I received a phone call that led to more enrichment of our Friday Morning Men's Fellowship leadership bench. "My name is Oliver Sale. Would you teach our Sunday school class this Sunday?" The conversation was not many more words than that.

I did not take long to answer. My policy when asked to speak anywhere was to accept whenever possible. I agreed to speak to the class. For starters, I asked Oliver if there was a flip-chart easel available. I explained I had a presentation for a one-time speaking engagement, and it had a lot more impact if I could draw a couple of simple diagrams.

That Sunday morning when I arrived at the church, they could not find an easel. It might have impressed Oliver when I went back to my car and pulled out my own easel. My IBM training was to be prepared for any contingency.

The Sunday school class was a typical mainline hybrid social club with various committees loaded with doctors, lawyers, businesspeople, and one college professor of note, Dr. Thomas Stanley, who had studied people of wealth and was the author of *The Millionaire Next Door*.

I preached the gospel, and I preached it clearly for maximum impact. I was trying to touch a nerve: the needs we face in this fast-paced, rat-race society in which we live. The gospel is for us, too. The problem with the rat race is that even if we win, we are still rats. The nerves I tried to touch were overloaded lives: debt, shallow relationships, loss of intimacy. One woman wept quietly. The message had touched her.

Somehow or other the class power brokers decided they liked me and asked me to come back. I did so for a year. I taught a series on the Ten Commandments, which is now on the Leadership Ministries website. In that series, I incorporated a key principle for interpreting the commandments as taught to me by Dr. Walter Kaiser. For instance, the negative command, "Thou shalt not kill," includes the opposite positive. So what would be the opposite positive of not taking a human life? Wouldn't it include not hoarding money while children all over the world are starving, not aborting babies? How about helping to educate young people through mission efforts?

On the positive end, the commandment includes doing everything we can to enhance human life. It is what Jesus said in the Sermon on the Mount: "You have heard that it was said to the people long ago, 'You shall not murder, and anyone who murders will be subject to judgment.' But I tell you that anyone who is angry with a brother or sister will be subject to judgment. Again, anyone who says to a brother or sister, 'Raca,' is answerable to the court. And anyone who says, 'You fool!' will be in danger of the fire of hell" (Matthew 5:21–22).

I used the passage from Jesus' Sermon on the Mount deliberately, because when I was young, a religious uncle was trying to tell us about leprechauns in the Irish storytelling tradition. In my precocious youth, I told him he was crazy. Boy, he got so mad at me. He looked at me and said, "You are a fool." That hurt deeply. I never forgot it.

"Do you see what Jesus is doing here?" I asked the class. "He is saying when He gave the command to not kill, He was including the sinful practices of broken and dysfunctional life destroying human relationships. Do not substitute religious activity for being obedient to the command to reconcile relationships. Do everything you can to make life better for people."

This is made crystal-clear as Jesus continued: "Therefore, if you are offering your gift at the altar and there remember that your brother or sister has something against you, leave your gift there in front of the altar. First go and be reconciled to them; then come and offer your gift. Settle matters quickly with your adversary who is taking you to court. Do it while you are still together on the way, or your adversary may hand you

━━━━━━━━━━━━━━━━

I preached the gospel,
and I preached it clearly for
maximum impact. I was
trying to touch a nerve:
the needs we face in this
fast-paced, rat-race society
in which we live. The gospel
is for us, too. The problem
with the rat race is that even
if we win, we are still rats.

━━━━━━━━━━━━━━━━

over to the judge, and the judge may hand you over to the officer, and you may be thrown into prison. Truly I tell you, you will not get out until you have paid the last penny" (Matthew 5:23–26).

Then I asked the class, "Can you imagine what the world would be like if we Christians were to obey all of the Ten Commandments?"

The class seemed to really appreciate the efforts I was making to teach them. The senior pastor visited the class and sometime later lamented to me privately over lunch that he, personally, did not get enough of that kind of teaching. He was about to retire from the denomination, so he risked transparency. It's no wonder the mainline denominations are shrinking in North America. The shepherds are malnourished.

Oliver and Joanne Sale

Oliver Sale and his wife, Joan, became friends to Suzanne and me and remained so until Joan died of cancer. Before she died, even before she knew her breast cancer had returned, they joined us on a trip to the Holy Land, which I talk about later in this book. A few years after Joan's death, Suzanne introduced her friend Joanne Eagle, a lovely widow, to Oliver Sale. Suzanne only made the introduction when she was sure that Oliver wanted a godly woman to marry. This was a marriage made in heaven. Oliver and Joanne have been faithful friends to Suzanne and me.

Oliver joined the FMMF and sat at Doug Lyle's table. We were making new table leaders as quickly as the Lord raised them up, and He raised them up when we continued to reach out to other men with the love of Jesus Christ.

Another providential turn of events came about the very first day in that Sunday school class. A young real estate broker stayed around after class while I was packing up my gear. He came right to the point. "I am Raymond Walker. I would like to have fellowship with you."

That was the start of an interesting and long-term relationship. Raymond is an entrepreneur. He goes where angels fear to tread. He loves to tell the story of how he started the Walker Companies by loading up a borrowed pickup truck when he spun out of a large multinational real estate company. He and an associate, John Wharton, developed a special value-added concept that helped companies find the best spot in the country to locate their industrial warehouse space. It was not easy, but they never gave up. Eventually they prospered, and finally they were able to sell the company for a premium.

Raymond started coming on Friday mornings and eventually became an excellent FMMF table leader.

Raymond has an enormous and compassionate heart. He and Huey Johnson, whom I also met in the Sunday school class, have been on many mission trips together. Huey, another successful entrepreneur, had developed a special product for retail-marketing shelving, and he enjoyed giving money to Christian missions.

Huey visited the FMMF with an African tribal chief who was studying at an Atlanta seminary. At breakfast after the fellowship, the chief made a statement I never forgot: "The problem with the church in America is that you have lost your intelligentsia. Those men are now in business, in government."

Raymond Walker

Wentzel Stewart

Assuming he was right, what was the solution?

One of our table leaders was Sandy Sanford, who perseveres as a leader in addition to building a successful highway concrete barrier construction firm. Sandy is also his own general contractor. When one of the men at Sandy's table, Wentzel Stewart, decided with his wife to homeschool their children, they needed a classroom. So Sandy rallied the table under his leadership to build them a classroom at their house. Wentzel's girls are now all grown up. One serves as a doctor; another as a PhD in marketing and communications at

Sandy Sanford

a major university. The Stewart children are college educated, productive members of our society. Intelligentsia, grass roots.

The church where I met Raymond Walker had a school connected to it, which was in decline. This became a cause for Raymond, who was growing in the faith and adding spiritual muscle after becoming a table leader and studying the Bible.

When a man like Raymond, with an entrepreneurial personality, is filled with the Holy Spirit and walks in faith, watch out! He took a year off from the Walker Companies focused on a struggling school that was revitalized and morphed into what is now the Wesleyan School, situated in northeast Atlanta.

Raymond helped with recruiting Zack Young, who had been the Director of Development for the Westminster Schools in Atlanta, to accept the position of headmaster at the Wesleyan School. For perspective on this outstanding educator, consider that the Westminster School was the top academically-rated private college prep school in Georgia.

Zack not too long ago gave me a tour through the Wesleyan School campus and emphasized the Christ-centered mission of the school. It was so impressive for me to realize that every square inch of that valuable property had been purchased by Raymond Walker and others he had mobilized, and was now filled with modern classrooms, labs, a performing arts center, and athletic facilities. Education with a biblical worldview is a ray of hope for our secular culture.

On the west side of Atlanta now sits the campus of Whitefield Academy. Whitefield got its start when Jeff Muir, one of our board of directors, recruited his college roommate, Dr. David Jones, an Atlanta dentist, to join his table at the FMMF. David joined the leadership team with his faith revitalized in the FMMF fellowship at Houlihan's.

David and his wife, Vesta, were serving on the board of the Mount Vernon Christian Academy. That school had been a wonderful experience for our family for grades seven through twelve. It was small by Atlanta standards, but it worked very well for our family,

Vesta and David Jones

because the school approached education with a Christian worldview compatible with ours.

I remember Dr. Roy W. Lowrie, a leader in Christian education, saying that we should be careful not to confuse young minds. It was imperative that what they are taught in school, a Christian worldview, is the same at home and at church. It was certain they would face a perplexing and cruel world soon enough.

David and Vesta were impressed by their family's experience at Mount Vernon Christian Academy, and as board members they wanted it to prosper. They started searching for ways to grow the school. David became the board chairman.

At the same time, there was a group of Christian couples from affluent northwest Atlanta who were meeting and praying for a good secondary school on the west side of the city. Headmaster Chuck Johnston, who had served at Trinity School for years, was a leader in that group.

David Jones and Chuck Johnston achieved something enormously strategic for the Atlanta community, although it seemed almost impossible. For David, his task was painfully arduous, but he effectively led the board, and they knitted a vision that combined the needs of the existing board at Mount Vernon School and the newest group of parents.

I met with David informally with my consulting hat and listened as he vented some of his frustrations with how some of the old-guard Christians behaved. It simply provided another opportunity for David to patiently exercise his faith. There is something about people of faith, borne out by church history, that makes them more ready to fight than to abide by Jesus' teachings to speak truthfully, to give soft answers that turn away wrath. Yet it is still true that "a gentle answer turns away wrath, but a harsh word stirs up anger" (Proverbs 15:1). David, the skillful professional, his wife, Vesta, and Chuck Johnston were able to follow the biblical teaching in bringing to reality the new Christian school.

Mount Vernon Christian Academy morphed into Whitefield Academy after our sons, Colin and Christopher, had graduated from Mount Vernon. Our son Joshua started in the sixth grade at Whitefield even before it had moved to its new campus. The new academy was named after the extraordinary Anglican preacher-evangelist George Whitefield, who was instrumental in the eighteenth-century Great Awakening in America. Since a good part of his ministry centered in Georgia, he was a great patron saint for the new school.

Chuck Johnston

Providentially, the Roman Catholic archdiocese of Atlanta had its eye on the Mount Vernon School property and bought it for three million dollars. As a result, Whitefield was launched with a lot of room to expand on a new property on the west side of Atlanta.

Raymond Walker and Dr. David Jones, both instrumental in those schools' development, were greatly mobilized in faith by the FMMF. They stand as a testimony to what happens when one man reaches out to another with the love of Jesus Christ. Whitefield Academy, especially, figures prominently in the development of our family and our family business.

The founding headmaster at Whitefield was Chuck Johnston, who had a long history in Christian education in Atlanta. Early in the development of Whitefield, Chuck let me help him assess candidates for teaching positions. We built a rapport.

His upper school principal was struggling in his career, and Chuck asked me if I could be helpful. I made a strategic decision to use the Life and Career Planning system developed for Leadership Development Company to serve the principal, Bob Neu. Money was thin, and I made it happen out of scarce operating funds. This was so effective in building Bob's confidence that he asked me if I could do anything for the students.

We knew that high school juniors and their families were very anxious about acceptance into college and the major selection process that followed, so we simplified our Life and Career Planning system for Whitefield Academy. Suzanne bravely got involved and facilitated small group meetings where the students discussed their unique talents, values, goals, and life purposes. We tested temperaments, values, and aptitudes with behavioral science tools. The combination of objective data and the dynamic of small-group discussion was delightfully effective.

At the end of the process, Suzanne met with each student, his or her parents, and Vesta Jones, the school college counselor, to discuss college issues in the context of our program. What an audacious success story this work was!

For twenty years, with five different headmasters, we served hundreds of families whose children went to college with at least a modicum of direction toward their life's work, their calling in life. This was all made possible by the courage and trust of men and women like David and Vesta Jones, Chuck Johnston, Suzanne White, and Scott Muir. Jill Langella, a mature woman of God. Jill was a trained counselor who worked with us at Whitefield and has continued the program. I am grateful for her courage and teamwork.

I worked with Scott Muir privately on a life and career plan to help him choose a college and college major that fit him. He went to Dartmouth, where he was an outstanding student and developed an interest in world religions. After graduation, he met with me again. He was thinking about graduate school but needed a year or two of work experience. He said, "Chris, I need to work for you." There was no equivocation and little hesitation on my part to hire him. His training gave us an absolute assurance that he could make a significant contribution, especially in life and career counseling.

Scott was a classic example of what we tell all our clients: hire an employer who will help you meet your objectives. Take creative control of your life. Scott jumped in and made a huge contribution to our success. He worked with the boys at Whitefield and on other private consulting engagements and became an invaluable staff teammate for the next two years, after which he went back to school to work on his PhD. Today, we still use the materials Scott developed for us.

Again, education with a biblical worldview is a ray of hope for our decadent culture. How do we get that worldview? The answer goes far back in time.

CHAPTER 30

Explore Our Roots

The late Sam King was a financial consultant who was zealous for Christ and had a heart for the people of God. He came to me in early 1998, and in his inimitable way said, "You are going to the Holy Land!"

He served on the board of Shoresh, a ministry based out of Jerusalem, whose mission is to make American Christians—and others—more aware of their Jewish roots. The Hebrew word *shoresh* means "roots." Today, we talk about Jews and Christians as though they are worlds apart. What irony.

Sam King

Jesus was Jewish. His disciples and other followers were Jewish. How did we go from there to the separation we have today between Jews and Christians? Well, that is what the Shoresh study tour is all about.

Sam was very convincing and made it financially easy for Suzanne and me. We signed up for a ten-day Shoresh study tour in the Holy Land. We experienced one of the most impactful excursions ever.

We went to New York a day before the flight to Tel Aviv, using the time to look up our original mentors, Dave and Dianne Balch, who were serving at Redeemer Church on the Upper East Side of Manhattan. That was where Suzanne and I first lived twenty-five years earlier. Now as we prepared for our trip to the Holy Land, Suzanne had a flintlike look and was determined to see Dave and Dianne. We had some unfinished business. We had never fully reconciled with them since our painful exit from Philadelphia eighteen years or so earlier. We had been polite with one another, but we had not been reconciled. Sure enough, the Lord loves this kind of mission, and He put us together.

When we entered the church on Sunday morning, there was Dianne right

Dave and Dianne Balch

in front of us as hundreds of people were congregating all around. Suzanne and Dianne found a place to talk, and I quietly found the Sunday school class where David was teaching. I slipped into the back row and hid behind another person. When Dave spotted me, he beamed with pleasure.

After church, we had lunch together and then visited with them in their apartment. That day was one of the sweetest times of reconciled fellowship we have ever experienced. My wise and devoted wife led the way. This was another epic point where Suzanne exercised her spiritual influence in our life and ministry. Because of my dysfunctional early childhood experiences, I hold grudges longer, but once we broke the ice, I asked the question for the four of us, "What lessons have we learned?"

We all confessed our sins to one another, and it was very good. Jesus was right there and smiling. "How good and how pleasant it is when God's people live together in unity!… For there the Lord bestows His blessing, even life evermore" (Psalm 133:1, 3).

After flying overnight, Suzanne and I met our hosts on Tuesday for the tour at Christ Church at the Jaffa gate in old Jerusalem.

Shoresh is part of an outreach to the Jewish people that was launched in the mid-nineteenth century from England. In 1842, God's people, including the outstanding disciple of Jesus, Lord Shaftesbury, sent Bishop Michael Solomon Alexander, a German-born Jew, the first Jewish leader of a Jerusalem church since AD 135, to the Holy Land. Alexander had taught Hebrew in England and was later ordained a rabbi there. He became a follower of Jesus in 1825 after meeting several Anglican clergymen who introduced him to the gospel.

Not surprisingly, he was ostracized by the Jewish community, but he remained proud of his heritage after coming to faith. Alexander was a lecturer of Hebrew and Rabbinic literature at Kings College in London when he was chosen to be the first bishop in the Middle East.

Alexander was an early advocate of the need for Christians to learn Jewish sources to better understand their faith. He was also convinced the people of Israel would return to their promised land, and once they were there, God would pour out His spirit on them and all mankind. And so am I. The apostle Paul wrote:

> I do not want you to be ignorant of this mystery, brothers and sisters, so that you may not be conceited: Israel has experienced a hardening in part until the full number of the Gentiles has come in, and in this way all Israel will be saved. As it is written:
> "The deliverer will come from Zion;
> he will turn godlessness away from Jacob.
> And this is my covenant with them
> when I take away their sins."
> As far as the gospel is concerned, they are enemies for your sake; but as far as election is concerned, they are loved on account of the patriarchs, for God's gifts and His call are irrevocable. Just as you who were at one time disobedient to God have now received mercy as a result of their disobedience, so they too have now become disobedient in order that they too may now receive mercy as a result of God's mercy to you. For God has bound everyone over to disobedience so that He may have mercy on them all. (Romans 11:25–32)

I believe before Jesus returns for the resurrection on that great and terrible day, the Jews will repent and become zealous evangelists.

Our study tour guide, David Pileggi, was an unforgettable charac-

David Pileggi

ter. When he and his wife, Carol, were in their twenties, they left Chicago for the Holy Land with little more than Carol's cello case. They went for the simple reason that God made David's life calling clear.

David loves the Jewish people and earned a master's degree at Hebrew University in Jerusalem. An imposing six-foot-two figure, he is a remarkable man. He shepherded us for the entire ten-day tour.

Our first stop was Caesarea, which is on the Mediterranean coast, north of Tel Aviv. We saw the architectural genius of Herod the Great, who built a harbor there with enslaved labor. Most of us are only exposed to one side of Herod, the paranoid power freak who had all the babies in Bethlehem killed because he was afraid of losing his kingdom. He was all of that, but he was also a visionary, a real estate developer, and an architectural genius. We all have a lot to learn.

David's style was to gather our group at a vantage point near a historic site and weave the biblical, the historical, and the archaeological threads together in a forty-minute lecture. Suzanne and I soaked it up like sponges.

The archaeological tell, or dig, at Megiddo, also known as Armageddon, was my most memorable experience from the tour. As we stood next to the tell, the Mediterranean was in sight a couple of miles to the west, and out in front of us was the Plain of Jezreel, where battles have been fought for nine thousand years over twenty-five civilizations.

Mount Carmel, where Elijah defeated the four hundred prophets of Baal, stretched out also to the west. As David talked, I had a wonderful feeling of being very small, not even a dot on the time line of history. And at the same time, I was reminded of God's grace. "But God demonstrates His own love toward us in this: While we were still sinners, Christ died for us" (Romans 5:8).

Everything in the Holy Land is muted. The supposed site of the Sermon on the Mount is not much more than a hill on the northwestern side of the Sea of Galilee, which is thirteen and a half miles long. In comparison, Mount Hermon, in the north, separating Israel from Lebanon, is 7,336 feet tall, the highest point in Israel.

In Bethlehem we were able to peer into the cave where it is said the Savior was born. In Jerusalem we were able to kneel on the rock called Golgotha, where the Son of God died for our sins. The site of the tomb from which Jesus rose from the dead is controversial, but David chose a site that has space for a service, where we celebrated Communion together with people from all over the world who were united by the life, death, and resurrection of Jesus Christ. It is truly an indescribable gift to be included in the family of God.

Our Shoresh tour and the in-depth studies I have done since are more evidence to me that the humble mission God called Suzanne and me to is the kind of work that is strategic. If we are to ever see a revival of authentic life-changing Christianity in the West, in the United States of America, this redemptive work must be rooted in the Old and New Testaments. That is what transforms lives. Getting back to our roots, we could see where Jesus worked with twelve men to show us how to minister His gospel.

On the return flight to New York, I had a seat next to a Hasidic rabbi. Hasidic Jews are recognized by their black clothing and strict beliefs and observances in militant opposition to modernity. In some ways, they resemble a Yiddish version of the Christian Amish.

We were not long in the air when this dear man developed a severe nosebleed, and there was blood all over the front of his clean white starched shirt. I fetched some towels from the restroom and assisted the rabbi as best I could. This gave us a rapport.

I was reading *The Jewishness of Jesus,* and I knew he could see the title of the book. He looked somewhat forbidding, but his embarrassed situation made him more approachable.

I asked him, "As a Jew, do you realize what you have?" I was thinking, "You have the remarkable privilege of being one of God's chosen people and all that it means."

His response to me was quick and definitive. In a strong Yiddish accent, he said, "Do I understand? Do I understand? I go to synagogue twice a day!"

Normally, I am very bold about personal evangelism, but my instincts told me this was a time to be only kind and helpful.

What we are dealing with today are twenty centuries of misinformation and horrific episodes of anti-Semitic atrocities.

I remembered from my studies with Dr. Hannah in church history how the Crusaders, as they crossed eastern Europe on the way to the Holy Land, wiped out a couple hundred thousand Jews along the way. The Holocaust and latent anti-Semitism seems ever ready to rear an ugly head with little provocation.

"I go to synagogue twice a day!"

Men have their favorite remedies for getting right with God. "I go to synagogue." "I go to church." "I try to keep the Ten Commandments."

Everything, though, is so far from the truth of what Jesus has done!

"I have come that they may have life, and have it to the full" (John 10:10).

"God made Him who had no sin to be sin for us, so that in Him we might become the righteousness of God" (2 Corinthians 5:21).

The study tour in Israel helped the Scriptures come alive for us like never before. It made a profound impact on our effectiveness as the founders of Leadership Ministries Inc. and Leadership Development Company. My teaching, for instance, now had more depth. It was better "rooted."

Now, we in the West, especially in urban America, seem to be somewhat in disarray. But Jesus is still working today.

———————◼————————

We all confessed our sins to one another, and it was very good. Jesus was right there and smiling. "How good and how pleasant it is when God's people live together in unity!… For there the Lord bestows His blessing, even life evermore."

PSALM 133:1, 3

———————◼————————

CHAPTER 31

A Silent Revolution

Jesus and his early followers were true revolutionaries. They were accused of turning the world upside-down. How in the world do we turn the world upside-down today?

Jesus is still working today through the silent revolution. That concept comes from George Gallup, the founder of the famous Gallup Poll. He was writing about the movement of men meeting quietly for the purpose of studying the Bible. I believe Leadership Ministries and the FMMF are part of this movement at work in our society.

Silently, under the radar, men are meeting in small groups much the way Jesus worked with a small group of men for three years. And when men meet together around the Word of God, long term in a low-pressure setting, and study the Scriptures, wonderful results can occur. They come to know Christ, the Lord of the universe.

Somewhere around 2002, Suzanne, seventeen-year-old Josh, and I traveled to the Billy Graham Training Center known as The Cove in Asheville, North Carolina. The speaker that weekend was George Barna, head of the Barna Research Group, who has a well-earned reputation for keeping his finger on the pulse of contemporary Christianity.

I took away two big things from that weekend seminar. First, leadership going forward in the United States will be more team-focused than star-centered. Leadership Ministries follows that trend. Second, the key element of growth is personal involvement with the Scriptures. This has been our focus now for more than forty years. We seem to be trending in the right direction.

But before we leave that weekend at The Cove, I must mention one other big thing about that weekend. Our son Josh attended every minute of every session. He seemed riveted on the wisdom that was being taught there. This was important for me because Josh is a very special part of our family, as I shared earlier. One of Josh's counselors said to me, "If we, as parents, put in the Word of God, it will come out."

Scott Henderson became a part of our FMMF. He was the president of the local alumni chapter of the college fraternity to which I belonged at the University of Connecticut. One day he asked me if I would speak at the chapter's monthly luncheon. Of course I said yes. My policy, adopted from my mentor Dick Woike in Philadelphia, was simple: I will speak to any group, providing I have complete freedom to speak my mind and heart.

My speech began with some stories from my days at IBM and my consulting practice with Leadership Development Company, where I had seen significant increases in personal and corporate productivity. This happens when people relate to each other positively and with trust, communicated effectively, and thus work together harmoniously. I contrasted those stories with cases of tragic business failures. Success, I emphasized, results from effective leadership. I spoke from personal experience with authoritative statistics from management science research.

Then I transitioned and explained how my life changed dramatically when business and professional men reached out to me with the love of Jesus Christ. I saw two men visiting from the fraternity's national headquarters slide down in their chairs at the back of the dining room, but I felt confident I was doing the right thing, because I had been given no parameters for my speech, and my host was beaming. Thus, I went on to explain how Arthur DeMoss and other men had led me to faith in Jesus Christ and how my life had changed. I had become a more effective leader in my marriage, family, and business life. I was proof positive of the impact of Christ on my life.

My talk was strong that day. I was speaking from my heart, from personal conviction and experience. I had learned the hard way that these stories have the most impact. The seventy-five men in the room seemed captivated. It was no wonder, for as Paul declared, "I am not ashamed of the gospel, because it is the power of God that brings salvation to everyone who believes: first to the Jew, then to the Gentile" (Romans 1:16).

As I was gathering my notes after the luncheon, a soft-spoken man lingered in the room long enough to speak to me privately. "My name is Solon Patterson," he said. "You mentioned Arthur DeMoss. I knew him quite well. I would like to meet with you again before too long."

Solon Patterson was the chairman of Montag & Caldwell, a leading investment advisory firm based in Atlanta and a trailblazer in its field. Solon introduced the first mutual fund in the state of Georgia. And, coincidentally, he was an early investor in Arthur DeMoss' company, National Liberty Corporation. Art had shared the gospel with Solon.

It took us a while to sync our calendars, but we eventually met in his Atlanta office. I will always remember the humility Solon showed when he bowed his head to pray with me in the privacy of his office. Although he was a devout member and leader in the Greek Orthodox Church. It was not long after this meeting that Solon joined my table on Friday mornings. He fit right in with the other business and professional men.

Over the years I have been privileged to see Solon's faith grow as we worked through the books of the Bible a paragraph or two a week. We were in the book of Romans when Solon reached out to his friend Berke Wilson. They were both members of the Homosassa Fishing Club in Homosassa, Florida, and Solon occupied space in a building that Berke's company managed. So, as was true in the first century, the gospel was flowing through these social and economic channels.

Our group at the Atlanta Homosassa Fishing Club in Florida. That's Solon Patterson seated to my right (front row).

Berke had visited the FMMF thirty years earlier. He was a young hotshot professional then, making deals in commercial real estate and too busy to stick. Now, thirty years or so later, life had dealt him some serious blows with a divorce and business reversals, and he was more open and teachable, when Solon invited him to the FMMF.

Berke Wilson

Berke joined Solon and me at our table. What a privilege to see hearts changed like light bulbs turning on when these men clearly understood that "all are justified freely by His grace through the redemption that came by Jesus Christ" (Romans 3:24).

Some weeks later Berke shared his testimony with the men on Friday morning and then at a luncheon at the Cherokee Town Club. It was humble and powerful. (Look for that testimony also on the LMI website.)

All this takes place usually quietly, silently, when one man reaches out to another man with the love of Jesus Christ. Thirty years earlier Art DeMoss had reached out to Solon Patterson. Thirty years earlier someone had reached out to Berke Wilson. But now it was time in God's sovereign grace that He would call these men to Himself. It was a beautiful thing for me to be part of all this teamwork, to be a leader. Paul wrote to the Corinthians about their fascination with celebrity preachers, "For we are co-workers in God's service… Each one should build with care" (1 Corinthians 3:9–10). No stars, just each man doing his part.

What a privilege to see men of Solon's and Berke's caliber, as well as Joe and Ken and others, in the fellowship together. These men, all from different church backgrounds, now understand more clearly God's plan of salvation. Meeting together on neutral ground at the Friday Morning Men's Fellowship has truly strengthened their faith.

Solon and his wife, Marianna, were brought up in the Greek Orthodox and Roman Catholic traditions, respectively. They have always been burdened by the cleavage resulting from the schism of AD 1050. Constantinople and Rome had their differences. Now Solon and Marianna are providing leadership in a movement to reunite these largest groups of Christians in the world, together totaling 1.5 billion people. They recently wrote a book, *East Meets West,* which chronicles their lives and their efforts to end the schism.

CHAPTER 32

Faithful Presence

Dr. James Davidson Hunter, a sociologist at the University of Virginia, developed his "faithful presence" thesis in describing what we need to focus on today in our urban culture in terms of Christian ministry. This observation from Hunter drives home the point (brace yourself for academic erudition): "In our tasks, the call of 'faithful presence' implies a certain modesty that gives priority to substance over style, the enduring over the ephemeral, depth over breadth and quality, skill and excellence over slick packaging or high production values."

Thus, faithful presence "would encourage ambition, but the instrumentalities of ambition are always subservient to the requirements of humanity and charity."

These thoughts are several levels of learnedness above what the average reader of this story is used to reading, including me. But stay with me as I explain how the men involved in the FMMF have built the model that sociologist Hunter described here.

1. "Faithful presence implies a certain modesty giving priority to substance over style." We deliberately meet in public restaurants that are not open for breakfast. This creates a modest environment where any man feels welcome, and we collect a dollar, which almost everyone can afford. But every week our table leaders and speakers make sure the men experience the Lord through substantial, yet

simple, biblical exposition. "Substance over style." The structure of the ministry is built with the needs of men in mind.

2. "The enduring over the ephemeral." Ephemeral means lasting for a brief time, the polar opposite of our FMMF culture. We have table leaders who have been leading men for more than thirty years. We have a man who has been ensuring a good logistical setup for almost forty years, and that man is Dave Dorries.

One early morning in the 1980s I was driving toward the Houlihan's restaurant in Buckhead. We had two or three new men every week. The fellowship was growing, and I was scrambling to train table leaders and stay ahead of the demand. Training consists of making sure the new table leaders know the model of table fellowship dynamics that Dr. Howard Hendricks had taught us. Practice makes perfect.

But we began having issues with logistics—the coffee, orange juice, and doughnuts provided at each meeting. This was starting to become a management problem. I prayed, Lord, if that man is there again this morning, please give me courage and the grace to ask him to help.

Dave Dorries had been coming early every week and sitting patiently while some volunteers scrambled to put things in order. All he needed was to be asked, and when I did, he jumped in and began to help.

That was in 1983. Since then, Dave has made sure that the other members of the team—the emcee, the speaker, and the table leaders—have nothing to worry about other than their main job of ministering to the men who show up. I cannot express my thanks enough for Dave's involvement over all these years.

One of Dave's major contributions to the mission was recruiting Jeff Terry to FMMF. Dave was there when Jeff was in a personal crisis with a divorce. By being there for Jeff, listening to this man in pain, he won his confidence, and Jeff started to attend the FMMF. Eventually, Jeff gave his heart to the Lord, became a table leader, and served as a board member. When Jeff chaired our annual Day of Golf, we doubled the revenue to $200,000.

Jeff Terry

Our leadership team circa 2011. Top row: Tom Eberle, Jeff Terry, Jeff Muir, Ted Kieler, Tom Wesley, Richard Owens, Bob Day, Colin White; Bottom row: Ken Thrasher, Brian Ranck, Chris White, Christopher White, Matt Lacey, Larry Corbitt.

Jeff is now an outstanding business leader in our community. His wife, Rachael, and Suzanne were very close.

Dave Dorries, a true leader, gathered a team of men around him so we always have backups. He went on to be a table leader and a member of our First Cut Leadership Forum. We met on the first Monday of every month to give God's work, God's Word, the "first cut" of our month. Robust disciples and leaders came out of this group. A large group of our first-cut men became table leaders, speakers, and service team members, who handled such necessities as A/V setup. This is how we have been able to add quality, skill, and excellence over the slick packaging or high production values Dr. Hunter talks about in his 2010 book *To Change the World*.

One day many years ago, when I was conducting a table leader training session, David Butler, who is now deceased, was there and serving as a board member. So he felt free to interject about my flip charts papering the walls. David felt the meeting was becoming too IBM-ish, and he said somewhat impatiently to the group, "Listen, just love and serve the men."

Dave Butler's admonition serves as a good balance to the case for best practices. But if table leaders do not strive for quality relational content, good skills, good questions, and excellence, then a good loving and serving heart will fall short.

One Friday morning I had to get up very early to get to a restaurant that was an hour away. Some men had spun out of our fellowship in

Buckhead and started their own in a retirement community. My bias toward freedom and encouraging men to take initiative, though, backfired in this case. When the leaders refused to come under our aegis and take the necessary training, we should have let them go. Instead, I accepted their invitation to speak that Friday. They had publicized my coming, and, sure enough, an old IBM buddy had shown up for the first time.

Steve, my friend, was apprehensive that morning. I could tell because when I extended the hand of friendship to him, his hand and his upper lip were wet. I prayed for God's grace.

My fifteen-minute testimony of God's grace in my life was fine. The men seemed engaged. The problem came when we went to a table and the table leader was a bomb, because he hadn't been trained in our 3P method. He defaulted to churchspeak and politics. It was awful, but it taught me a good lesson.

If men are not open to come under the distinctives we have had to learn the hard way, over a long period of time, that help men to grow, then move on. "Move with the movers."

CHAPTER 33

Planning for the Future

Our son Christopher became the founding Leadership Ministries, Inc. board chairman, and he has been a table leader for many years. He met Alec Dicks when they partnered in getting their MBA degrees at the University of Georgia Terry School of Business. They did this after both had put some scratches on their football helmets (practical business experience).

It was not long before Alec joined Christopher at his table on Friday mornings. Christopher knows the business. Alec is with Gartner, a leading research and advisory company. Planning is their forte. They help companies plan their worldwide technologies for the future. Alec grew through the fellowship, and he eventually spun out with his own table. Then he came on our board of directors and brought a new level of professionalism to our thinking and planning.

Alec Dicks

To ensure the endurance of the ministry, under Alec's leadership we began to look to the future. Through a series of gatherings of table leaders and off-site overnight retreats with the board, under Alec's skillful guidance, we started to formulate a strategic plan in preparation for succession. We needed to answer this question: How can we ensure we will pass our distinctive philosophy and system of developing men to the next generation of leadership?

The thoughts from these discussions have been distilled to the following purpose statement and statement of values.

Purpose Statement: The purpose of Leadership Ministries is to equip men to be faithful leaders in their marriages, families, businesses, and wider communities and to teach them to equip others to be the same.

Guiding Beliefs:

- This country needs strong families, where a disciplined, loving, and creative atmosphere shapes our children's character.
- This country needs strong marriages, where a man listens to his heart and leads from within, serving his wife and family from the strength of the Holy Spirit.
- This country needs strong businesses built on a foundation of truth, integrity, and service and led by men who understand a scriptural model of male servant leadership.
- This country needs a rebirth of society where courageous men will lead a charge against the social ills of the day by becoming all that God intends them to be, regardless of the criticism they may face.
- This country needs mature, experienced men to mentor younger men for the next generation of leadership.

Leadership Ministries Core Values

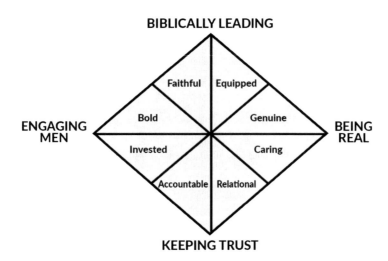

We offer encouragement to men, and we value biblical fellowship that connects and makes a practical and righteous impact on life's institutions, especially marriage, families, and businesses. Our vision is to see men all over the United States of America and the world rise proactively in exponentially growing numbers to the challenge of biblical leadership.

Biblically Leading

We are convinced the Bible is God's written will, revealed for our lives. We have a passion for God's word as "all Scripture is God-breathed and is useful for teaching, rebuking, correcting and training in righteousness, so that the servant of God may be thoroughly equipped for every good work" (2 Timothy 3:16–17). As leaders in the body of Christ, we know when we look at life and at the world through a biblical lens, we can embrace our God-given callings and lead confidently. Our aim is to teach the Word of God to faithful men who will then be qualified to teach it to others.

Being Real

Men are hungry for reality. We believe men need to know the Truth, and we are called to get real with them by being genuine as we share our own struggles as husbands, fathers, friends, and professionals. We admit we don't have easy answers. We do know, however, our relationship with Jesus Christ makes all the difference in our lives. We are caring enough to allow the Holy Spirit to guide us as we meet men where they are in their own lives.

Keeping Trust

We will build lasting relationships with men through a long-term, low-pressure approach. When we do not betray our fellow men, we build and keep a foundation of trust. We will hold each other accountable to our word and embody Proverbs 27:17: "As iron sharpens iron, so one person sharpens another."

Engaging Men

Because of God's grace in our lives and the heritage of courageous leaders who came before us, we are called to engage other men with a bold spirit. We actively invite and welcome men to Christian fellowship in order to emulate Christ. We take an active interest and are deliberate about how to be involved in the men's lives whom God has called us to serve.

At the heart of Leadership Ministries is the Friday Morning Men's Fellowship. This forum is our outreach to Atlanta's business and professional men. We remain steadfast in keeping the mission focus of Leadership Ministries: to develop and equip men to lead in their marriage, family, and business.

As Ken Thrasher noted in a mission report: "In 1987, the Friday Morning Men's Fellowship changed my world. I used to see things through my own lens—what I could do for God. Through this ministry, including making it my highest giving priority, I now understand God does not 'need me,' but He has given me a purpose to reflect His glory in my marriage, family and business. Thankfully, now my own sons participate with other young men in this fellowship. Through the viewpoint of this next generation, we are all bringing the light of Jesus Christ into their daily lives and the lives of others."

Jody Daniel Newman, a regular at the On the Border FMMF for several years, described the effect of studying Scripture. "Over the years, we've traversed Philippians, Acts, Job, Romans, Hebrews, and various other books. We go slow—a few lines per week. Our table worked through the book of Matthew for two years. A few times during these sessions, I've had what are, to me, utter epiphanies.

"I remember a time, for example, feeling like 'everyone else' was hearing the voice of the Creator—like Moses or David or a prophet or an enlightened guy at FMMF. I had never 'heard' any such responsive voice, and I wondered if I ever would and why. One Friday at the table, while we were unpacking some text, a short passage beamed with clarity. I can only say it 'sounded' like 'hearing' a 'voice.' At that moment, I wondered no more. I simply stopped expecting to hear another kind of voice."

The table is the primary training platform on Friday mornings. Each table leader has volunteered and has been formally trained to facilitate discussion of God's Word and its practical application to men's lives. The FMMF opens with ten to fifteen minutes of unstructured social time. Afterward, guests are introduced, and a speaker gives a short talk from the Bible that is usually part of a series. On some Fridays men are also led to give their testimonies to provide them an opportunity to share their faith and lead other men to Christ. These table leaders and speakers form the leadership team and continue to develop new leaders.

In addition, Leadership Ministries staff lead a First Cut meeting each month for men who desire to delve deeper into discipleship training. These meetings consist of six to twelve men, which is similar in size to a FMMF table, and sessions occur over a period of six to twelve months.

In 2012, we began a six-month mentoring program fashioned after Regi Campbell's Radical Mentoring, where senior executives from FMMF invite younger men into their homes to study God's plan for their businesses, marriages, and personal lives. This ministry is a natural extension of Friday mornings and allows faithful men to have their own impactful ministry to others who are seeking wisdom and best practices in applying their faith to their daily life.

The men who are currently mentoring younger men are:

Alan Bullock

Alan Bullock: Alan began his mission of mentoring young men in their Christian faith through the Radical Mentoring program in 2014. He has been a longtime participant in the FMMF as well as being active in the Fellowship of Christian Athletes at the University of Georgia. After graduating from the University of Georgia in 1975, he formed a commercial real estate company, Bullock Mannelly Partners Inc., which focuses on commercial development and investment banking. In addition to serving on the governing boards of various real estate–related agencies, Alan is an active member of the UGA Terry Business School Board and enjoys mentoring UGA students and athletes. He has been married for forty-five years to his high school sweetheart, Cindy, and they have three grown children and four grandchildren.

Ken Thrasher: Ken is a founding partner and chairman emeritus of Bennett Thrasher LLP, an IPA Top 100 in the US CPA and consulting firm. Ken and Cathy, his wife of forty-three years, live in Vinings and have three adult sons and five grandchildren. Ken has attended the FMMF since 1987 and serves on the boards of directors of LMI and the Leadership Ministries Foundation Inc. He also serves on the board of directors of Atlanta Habitat for Humanity, Southern Federal Tax Institute, Langham Partners USA, and UGA Terry College Alumni. A University of Georgia graduate, he earned a bachelor's degree in business administration and a master's degree in accounting.

Bob Voyles

Bob Voyles: Bob is a longtime participant in the FMMF, and we first met while he was engaged in our Life and Career Planning process. Since moving to Atlanta in 1980, Bob has been involved in the commercial real estate industry, first as a transactional attorney at a major Atlanta law firm, and later on the principal side for a national development firm. More recently Bob started his own commercial development and asset management firm, which is now eighteen years into its start-up. Bob has been married for forty-six years to his sweetheart for life, Belle, and they have four grown children and eight grandchildren. Bob has also led numerous mentoring groups over the past ten years and is called to this ministry.

Our bench of mentors is deep in both discipleship skill and successful business experience. The men love this dimension of our ministry. This relates to the example of William Tyndale, the sixteenth-century reformer of the Roman Catholic Church, whose English translation of the Bible was the first to use the printing press and provide the Scriptures to common people in their own language. Though Tyndale died a martyr's death for heresy, his work was monumental and paved the way for the King James Version of the Bible, which drew heavily from Tyndale's translation. He realized "how that it was impossible to establish the lay people in any truth except the Scripture were plainly laid before their eyes in their mother tongue."

It has been almost five centuries since that first English translation appeared. The Bible is widely available in our society and occupies a place in many of our homes. But as I have observed before, most American business and professional men do not view the Scriptures as relevant to their God-ordained roles as leaders of their marriages, families, and businesses.

Men have a special, unique role. To carry it out successfully, they first need Jesus Christ in their lives, and then to be fully equipped to carry out their roles. That is what Leadership Ministries is called to do: develop leaders for the body of Christ.

CHAPTER 34

A Man Tells What It's Like

The following story is a candid, real-life example that illustrates what we have been talking about. Charlie Paparelli heads up a ministry to the technology business community. He is an investor and businessman who got his start thirty years ago at the FMMF. The following was originally published on Charlie's blog as part of an ongoing series called "Reimagine Your Life." To read the rest of the series, go to www.paparelli.com and subscribe.

My First Bible Study—Charlie Paparelli

"What are you looking for?" Kathy asked as she saw me rummaging through the bookshelves in our bedroom.

"I am looking for a Bible," I said.

"A Bible? Why do you want a Bible?" she asked in disbelief.

"I am going to a Bible study in the morning," I said.

"You are going to a what?" she asked. "You are going to AA every night, and now you are going to start going to a Bible study?"

"Do we own a Bible or not?" I asked.

"My sister gave me a Bible when I was a kid. I think it's on a bookshelf in the basement."

I went downstairs and found it. It was an ugly green book with dried, swollen pages. At one time it must have been soaked in water and later dried out. It would barely rate as used—acceptable on the Amazon book condition scale. But I found it.

I was ready to attend my first Bible study.

At 7:00 a.m. I walked through the front doors of the restaurant. I was greeted by a man my age. He was quick to welcome me and introduce himself. "Welcome to the Friday Morning Men's Fellowship. Is this your first time?"

Charles Paparelli

He had me fill out a name tag and then pointed me to the coffee and doughnut bar laid out for the guests. It was a friendly crowd. A couple of men introduced themselves, but I was more interested in keeping a low profile.

After all, I had no idea how to conduct myself in a Christian fellowship. I didn't know what to expect. Would they call on me to speak? Ask me to read the Bible or, worse yet, tell them why I had come in the first place? What was I going to say? "I'm looking for my higher power? Have you seen him?"

Chris White, the leader of the gathering of approximately forty men, called the meeting to order. He asked everyone to find a seat. Then he said, "Welcome, men. Thanks for getting out of bed so early to hear the Word of God and discuss it. We are here to learn more about our Lord and Savior Jesus Christ. For those who are here for the first time, our format is simple. I'll choose a selected reading from the Bible and then speak for ten minutes on the passage. Then we'll get together in small groups to discuss what we've learned and how it might apply to our lives. If you don't have a regular table, please see John over there, and he will assign you to one."

Then Chris said, "Please turn to Matthew 6, verses 1 through 10."

I sat there frozen.

I had no idea how to follow those instructions. What was Matthew? Where was Matthew? Who was Matthew? And what did the numbers mean? I didn't want to look stupid, so I opened the Bible to about the middle and looked like I was reading something. What I was doing was hoping nobody was watching me. I didn't want to look incompetent, but I needed help.

He did what he said he would do. He read the Bible. It seemed like everybody except for me was following along with him. Then he talked about what he had just read. I don't remember any of it.

When Chris concluded his remarks, he said, "Okay, let's head to our tables."

As instructed, I went to see John. He was kind to me, as I expected. He showed me to a table with five men I'd never met and asked me to introduce myself. Then each of the men in turn stood and shook my hand. The leader of the small group thanked me for coming and welcomed me. He said, "We are glad you're here. Our format is simple. I'll ask questions about what Chris read and talked about, and each of us will have a chance to share our thoughts."

And with that short introduction, I started my first Bible study.

Before he asked any questions, the table leader asked me why I chose to attend that day. I said, "Bill Leonard sent me here. I was interested in learning more about God, and he recommended this meeting."

Then the leader asked for prayer requests. Each man gave an update of what was going on in his life. I was struck by how transparent these men were about their lives, families, and business challenges. Some of the stories were horrible. Parents with cancer, wayward kids, marriages not working, no job or income, bad bosses, and the list went on. I was thinking, "I'm in AA and can't seem to figure out what I'm going to do professionally, but my wife and kids love me. I'm in pretty good shape." But I didn't share any of this. I was there to observe and learn.

Then the leader asked a man to pray for the prayer requests.

I'd never heard a prayer like he prayed. It was from the heart and it was free-form. He was simply in a conversation with God. Until that moment, I'd only heard people read or recite prayers from a prayer book. This guy was talking to God like he was sitting at the table with us.

"What did you think about the reading?" the leader asked.

I listened as these men shared their insights and struggles.

It was like a book club discussion but far more personal. The more the men at the table shared, the more comfortable I became. These guys are just like me. They are struggling with life and searching for answers.

They're here because they believe God has the answers. And they think the answers to their questions can be found in the Bible.

At the end of our time together, each of the men thanked me for coming and asked me to join them next week.

I liked these guys.

They were not like the people I was meeting while networking in the community. They were authentic and transparent, unguarded. I wanted to be authentic and transparent. Maybe this was a place where I could be that way. Maybe, just maybe, this was something I should attend every week.

Could I trust them?

Could I tell them the truth?

I said, "I'm looking for an introduction to my higher power. Can you point me in the right direction?"

Charlie Paparelli is president of High Tech Ministries, an angel investor, and a blogger. Twice each week, email subscribers to his blog receive his thoughts on being a successful entrepreneur and Christian leader.

CHAPTER 35

Building a Great Team

For several years we organized a group of six company owners we called the CEO Forum. Its purpose, consistent with our overall mission, was to provide these business owners with a sounding board to allow them to confidentially discuss the issues on their minds and hearts. How could they better provide righteous leadership in the sphere in which God had placed them?

Very often, the issues were more family related than business related. A common challenge was their teenagers. And that holds true for most families.

When one of our younger business owners had dated a woman for several years and had not yet proposed marriage, Pat Capuano, who owned a printing company, laid down the law to this young man. He said, "You know, Tom, we are not made that way. You need to get married or let her go." It was not much longer before the young business

Tim Gartland

owner proposed and they were married. Last time I checked, they had three children. The point is, older and wiser men can mentor the younger through the FMMF program and the venues growing out of it.

Looking back on that experience with the CEO Forum, I believe our greatest deficit was not being truthful enough when we saw problems. Two cases had the same thread, the same common denominator: adding overhead too quickly and branching out into ventures where you do not have competency. They were bad moves for both owners, and we should have been more forthright in our counsel.

From a purely financial standpoint, this is under-capitalization. Bill Carter, one of the founding members of this work, advised us, "Never underestimate the power of capital."

I agree from personal experience. Suzanne and I had a built-in governor that controlled the speed with which we tried to grow. We built the equity in our lives through sweat and hard work. We were both hardwired that way. Nothing heroic, but the bottom line was, with all due modesty, we were just a great team. By God's grace we both had temperaments that allowed us to wait. Waiting is good! Delay gratification. We always dreamed of having a walk-in closet. We were almost seventy before we saw it happen.

Tom Eberle

While I have been helpful to men in thinking through their life- and career-planning issues, I found it impossible to think about this mission in any kind of detached and objective manner. Tactical matters and operational issues took all my time, and this was my baby. With Suzanne's partnership and other faithful partners, we birthed the baby. I liked being in charge of building the culture. We needed help.

In 2006, the Lord sent a special man to help us, but he came to us first as a client. Tom Eberle was from Nashville, Tennessee, and he was a man in transition—our specialty. After helping to shut down his family's leather tanning business, an industry that is now almost entirely offshore, Tom needed a new tack for his life and career, which made him a perfect fit for our Life and Career Planning service. When a client comes in from out of town, there is an intensive three-day schedule. Suzanne and I usually take the client to dinner one night. When we brought Tom back to his hotel after dinner, Suzanne and I talked, and we agreed Tom was an exceptional man.

One thing led to another, and Tom developed a model, a FMMF in Brentwood, Tennessee, near Nashville, patterned after the work in Atlanta. Tom became a friend and a confidant, and over several years he helped me to come around to where I could play an active role in seeing that our work did not evaporate as I grew older.

His patience and intelligent guidance were a wonder to behold. He pointed out to me that I was a monomaniac. If men are not being discipled to follow Christ, we are not doing anything worthwhile, as far as I am concerned. Tom was a ballast of support as we entered some turbulent waters.

This came into play especially during the Great Recession of 2007–2009, which put everyone under great stress. And I made relational errors within the board and staff. The big problem was making tactical personnel decisions without a framework of a well-thought-out long-range plan. We had hired some younger staff members to help with the increasing number of men attending the FMMF. We also wanted to reach younger men as the founding generation aged. Some young staff wanted to succeed me as the CEO, but their marriages were not strong enough to sustain that responsibility. This created a crisis that we did not handle well. None of us did, but I take full responsibility.

I asked Tom to facilitate a peacemaking process. But at an executive committee meeting when Tom was going to lay out the plan, a board member who preferred a therapeutic approach shut down the conversation. He would have none of a biblically based conflict resolution process; he wanted to coach one of the younger men personally. Our lack of experience and spiritual immaturity were tested, and we were found wanting.

So, for the next two years, we suffered through the pain of meeting as an executive committee without the rapport we once had. The Lord taught me a great lesson about strategic planning, communication, staff selection, and conflict resolution that I will never forget. He disciplined me.

And have you completely forgotten this word of encouragement that addresses you as a father addresses his son? It says,

"My son, do not make light of the Lord's discipline,
and do not lose heart when He rebukes you,
because the Lord disciplines the one He loves,

and He chastens [KJV scourgeth] everyone He accepts as His son."

Endure hardship as a discipline; God is treating you as his children. For what children are not disciplined by their father? If you are not disciplined—and everyone undergoes discipline— then you are not legitimate, not true sons and daughters at all. (Hebrews 12:5–8)

God whipped me good!

The time that seemed wasted provided more clarity and reasonableness. Then we moved very carefully toward a day when it would be possible for me to step down and allow the younger generation to guide the mission.

We had made one especially good move before the debacle of 2006–2008 that has proven to be pivotal, even if somewhat fortuitous. Again, we did not really know what we were doing. I was in the cockpit, and my decisions were pragmatic, but they lacked professional counsel and any experience. No one on the board would come on too strong. They were faithful to me as the founder, for the most part, and tried to be supportive. One thing was sure, though: we needed capital if the work were ever to pass to the next generation.

Because of the cyclical nature of giving to the work, the little repetitive revenue to LDC, and the need to think more strategically, the board approved my suggestion to form a foundation that would give us some staying power.

We hired a consultant who taught us the rudiments of the process. After all the PowerPoint slides were finished in his presentation, for me, it came down to one issue: who would be the lead donor? When you have a lead donor, the campaign backfills around that bedrock foundation.

The men on the board with financial acumen helped us come up with a $1.5 million goal for establishing the foundation. Again, the purpose was to steady the work, to give it more sustainability, to provide a more strategic approach to what we were doing, and to allow us to plan for the future.

Jim Gray

While Jim and Claudia O'Hanlon lived in Atlanta, Jim had taken full advantage of our capacities here. He and Claudia were solid as a rock in our corner. He became a very faithful disciple of the Lord, and Claudia,

196

like Suzanne, was a full partner with her husband.

After Jim and Claudia moved to Richmond, Virginia, where he headed up the nuclear power division of Dominion Power, he attended a Prison Fellowship meeting in Washington, DC. There, he met Jim Gray of Atlanta and referred him to us. Jim, a blue-chip man, had a career with IBM and was an army colonel. He had many years with Prison Fellowship, and now he was the national chaplain for the Veterans of Foreign Wars (VFW). He has proved to be a pillar in our Atlanta FMMF, a supporter of the whole mission, and a faithful table leader.

Claudia and Jim O'Hanlon

Who would be the lead donor? I kept turning that question over in my mind and praying for an answer.

Jim O'Hanlon came to my mind. He had established a charitable family foundation, and he knew us well. I called him about a week before the next board meeting. "Jim, we are establishing a foundation for long-term sustainability of the work of Leadership Ministries Inc. The consultants have advised us that the first thing we need is a lead donor who will pledge twenty percent of the campaign goal, and that would be $300,000."

I confess I could not believe I was asking for that much money, but the Lord gave me the boldness. I held my breath before Jim replied.

"Chris, let me talk to Claudia," he said. "I will be back to you in a couple of days."

On Wednesday morning, Jim called me and said, "Claudia and I have talked, and we would like to pledge $300,000 over the next five years: $60,000 per year." I almost fell out of my chair.

At the board meeting on Thursday afternoon, I tried to keep a straight face. When we got to the foundation on the agenda, I said, as calmly as possible, "Men, I called Jim O'Hanlon and asked if he would be our lead donor. He called yesterday and said that he and Claudia would like to pledge $300,000."

The conference room exploded. No one had believed we could do it. That was probably a great Churchillian moment in our history. Jim was Roosevelt, and I was Churchill, with my back against the wall on a phone call begging for mercy—with a scotch by my side.

Jim became the founding chairman, and over the next two years he regularly flew to Atlanta at his own expense and we made joint calls to faithful friends who had the ability to support the foundation. The pledges rose to $750,000, half of our goal.

Jim had a very simple sales pitch. "When Chris asked me to be the lead donor, I thought about what this ministry had done for me. They led me to Jesus Christ and eternal life. It is the least I can do." When he was turned down, with typical modest New England humility, he would simply say, "I don't understand."

Between Jim's trips to Atlanta, Ken Thrasher and Jeff Muir kept up the momentum. One of the most rewarding results was that people outside of our circle who are knowl-

Christopher White

edgeable about ministry development were impressed with this strategic move.

The Leadership Ministries Foundation played a key role in, first of all, allowing us to weather the Great Recession, to work through the development of a strategic plan, and to be able to land Suzanne and me softly into the next phase of our lives.

The work is now led by a board of directors, initially chaired by our oldest son, Christopher, who was succeeded by Ken Thrasher. Our second son, Colin, who is a CFA, became the treasurer. I do not serve on this board. Peace!

What a joy to see my sons and the other men carrying on this work. And there is much more ahead for them and other faithful partners.

CHAPTER 36

At the Right Time

David Fritts has been involved in the FMMF since early on. We struck up a friendship that developed into a mutually beneficial relationship. He became a client of LDC as well as a regular part of our First Cut Leadership Forum, and he and his wife, Lisa, became friends to Suzanne and me.

An unforgettable memory having little to do with our main mission was an apple pie Lisa made for us. It was so delicious, an apt metaphor for our friendship and fellowship.

When I met David, he was in the mortgage origination business, but after I got to know him and had the benefit of data from our Life and Career Planning tools, I encouraged him to expand his consultative skills to help clients develop wealth. He had invaluable experience as an air force pilot, as well as a successful career in healthcare information technology sales. He had the right combination of brains and drive. So with the empirical data from his track record and the objective data from the various instruments we use—especially temperament, aptitudes, and values—I urged him more aggressively.

From that point, David went on to become a certified financial planner and helped to make several middle-class millionaires. He has been an immense help to me with informal counsel when I have struggled with my own financial decisions. He is highly objective and a real friend in these matters. We have the bond of common experience. We both have experienced the challenge of starting small and seeing the Lord build the house.

Early in 2014, David asked me to meet a friend of his who needed my ministry. That in itself was a high compliment of trust from a friend. I have always seen an opportunity to consult with other men as a privilege.

We met at Joey D's steakhouse in Sandy Springs for lunch. Fortunately, I had just received my hearing aids after Suzanne harassed me into purchasing them. This was precipitated by my effort to fake a conversation with a woman at a cocktail party. The background noise had been deafening, and I could not hear a word she said. I tried to read her lips, and I got caught. "What did you hear me say?" she asked in an aggravated tone. That was the proverbial straw that broke the camel's back.

With my hearing aids firmly in place, I arrived at the restaurant and met David. "This is my friend, Steve Weidman," he said.

Never, in all the years I have been in this business, have I met a man who looked so hurt. He had obviously met some devastating circumstance.

Steve Weidman grew up not too far from where I did in Connecticut, which gave us some common ground to start with. He had a successful career in labor law with a law firm and with Reynolds Aluminum, and he was the chief labor negotiator at Harley-Davidson Company in Milwaukee, Wisconsin, before recently retiring.

He and his wife, Donna, a childhood sweetheart, had been married for forty-five years. Now retired, they had it all planned. They would move to Atlanta to be near their children and grandchildren, and the picture was completed with a great getaway cottage on Hilton Head Island, South Carolina.

Six weeks before our meeting at Joey D's, it had snowed in Atlanta. Donna, a good Yankee woman, had decided to go out and shovel the snow off the walkway. When she came back into the house, she complained of pains in her midsection. The pains persisted for a couple of weeks, and Steve persuaded her to go to the emergency room. The doctors discovered she had advanced cancer.

Sixteen days later Steve's best friend and partner for forty-five years was gone! The shock and sorrow staggered him.

I prayed for Steve constantly. Let him trust me, I asked the Lord, knowing what Steve needed was authentic Christian fellowship around the Word of God.

Steve had bowed his knee to the Lord during the sixteen days between Donna's diagnosis and her departure from this earth. Now his faith needed to be nourished with men he could connect with and good, solid medicine from the Great Physician.

The medicine Jesus prescribed came from the book of Job. We were studying Job at my table. Steve jumped into the Scripture with all the considerable intellectual, disciplined power he could bring. He knew Job could help him. Every week Steve brought special insight to our table discussions. He put roots down. He was growing.

After a year or so I asked him to give his testimony. It was beautiful. Look for it on the Leadership Ministries website: "Steve Weidman Testimony."

Steve and I met on Friday mornings after the FMMF, and before long he saw an opportunity to serve me and the ministry. We talked about succession, for by then I had been leading the work for thirty-seven years. Several key men were ready to take over in a new board-led ministry model, but the business simply needed a shove.

And we had the right man who knew how to do just that. One Friday morning we met in our boardroom to talk about the future. I started to hem and haw, but Steve had been in such situations before with tough labor negotiators. He used his experience, his bold personality, and his love for me and the ministry to serve us.

"Chris, you are seventy-five years old!" He gave no quarter. That did it. Reality!

Mason Zimmerman, a prominent real estate developer and thirty-year FMMF veteran, helped us with the succession strategy. At the next board meeting, I asked Steve to join the board and lead us through the transition. He did so, and the new board of directors conducted a professional search. When they came down to three candidates, they let me back into the process.

Mark Maynard was bracketed by two candidates who had PhDs, but Mark had the track record. He stood out as a man with a strong

Mason Zimmerman

Renée and Mark Maynard

marriage, a twenty-year record of faithful Christian mission, an ability to raise money, and an innate ability to work in a board-led ministry. I had ascertained this by using our Life and Career Planning tools.

When asked, I cast my vote for Mark after Suzanne and I had met with Mark and his wife, Renée. Suzanne agreed. We saw a couple who were a true team, just as we were a team.

In January 2018, I became founder emeritus, and Mark became president and CEO. The ministry is now under the new board structure with Mark as the president and Jeff Adams as the current board chair.

CHAPTER 37

In Her Memory

Shortly after I stepped down from leading Leadership Ministries, Suzanne was diagnosed with a malignant tumor in her small intestine. This type of cancer is rare; most intestinal cancer is farther down in the colon. Surgery and six rounds of chemo seemed to heal her. The scans were clean.

Suzanne did everything she could to stay alive. She worked out at LA Fitness five days a week, she kept to a strict diet, ate blueberries, and made a colorful salad with lean chicken or fish for us every night. But for the next two years we found ourselves in a vicious cycle: clean scan… check again six months later to find that the cancer had returned with reinforcements… increase the rounds of chemo… clean scan… wait a couple of months… check again.

Finally, Dr. Patel, the surgeon, reported, "The cancer is all over." It was decision time!

Dr. Bachman, head of palliative care at St. Joseph's Hospital, lovingly helped us to understand our options. Suzanne was reflective.

"I have lived seventy-eight years. I have three good boys who know the Lord: Christopher, Colin, and Joshua. And our work is done," she said. "The ministry is in good hands, with our sons involved. I am ready to go home." There was no doubt in her mind she would be with the Lord. For encouragement, we read more about heaven, the resurrection, and the new heaven and the new earth in Randy Alcorn's 2004 book, *Heaven*.

Logically, it made no sense to stay on the offensive. We decided on hospice at home. On the sunny afternoon of October 17, 2020, with her three sons, me, and her nurse, Maryan, surrounding her bedside, Suzanne breathed her last.

She heard Jesus say to her, "Well done, good and faithful servant! You have been faithful with a few things; I will put you in charge of many things. [Probably, I guess, this will include decorating and aesthetics—but this time with a bigger budget.] Come and share your master's happiness" (Matthew 25:23).

The White Family

Thinking about Suzanne and our life together for fifty-two years, I not only loved my wife, but as we came to know Christ together and grew together and worked together, I also grew to increasingly respect her. Fifty-three years earlier, when I made my clumsy marriage proposal, she had responded, "Okay, I will take care of everything." And she did.

Suzanne was one gutsy girl. Whether it was about raising a family, moving out of her dream house, adopting Josh, moving to the South, whatever the challenge, she sought the Lord's guidance and followed Him. She was a good wife and mother and my partner. I love her. I cherish my memories of our life together.

At her memorial service, the three boys, her friend and pastor Ewan Kennedy, and I all spoke. Josh expressed his gratitude this way: "She gave her life so that I could have a life." He spoke for all of us who knew her.

CHAPTER 38

In Their Own Words

The men who have shared in our ministry come from many walks of life and have joined in the work at widely different points in their lives. I asked several of them to describe their involvement and what it has meant to them, thus, sometimes they address me in what follows. Some wives have also added a little of their own perspective.

The following stories show what lies at the heart of the Friday Morning Men's Fellowship and offer insight and inspiration.

Chad Boles, Atlanta, On the Border FMMF

The funniest thing happened on the way to work several years ago. I reached out to my friend Mike while searching for a nearby men's Bible study.

He replied, "There's one right next to your office."

I said, "Is it new?"

"No, it's been there thirty years."

After I chided myself for not knowing, I made the mental commitment to be there the next Friday. Since the first time I walked through the door, I knew from the man-sized handshakes, a doughnuts and coffee bar, and the purposefulness of each man I met, this would be the place for me. Christ intends for us to live a life filled with peace that comes from the rigorous academic study of the Bible, weekly fellowship with men seeking the same peace, constant prayer, and the principles taught through Christ's love. It's all about the journey, right? FMMF provides a platform for internalizing the road map of how to be a better man, father, leader, and colleague. Of how to get through the summits and the valleys of the journey.

Chad Boles

The journey? Man, I wish wisdom was cheaper.

Each Friday morning I haul myself to a bar, a diner, and an academy, all rolled into one, where I am surrounded by energetic, bright community leaders who are struggling with the same questions King Solomon wrestled with thousands of years ago. Man isn't so much different now than he's ever been. But Christ is the same as He ever was, and He's always there.

Bobby Norwood, Managing Director, Investment and Finance Team, Bullock Mannelly Partners Real Estate Company

I first came to FMMF in 2008. I didn't know what to expect. I sat at a table led by Dan Gardner and full of guys I knew from high school and college. The message on the first day was challenging and direct (Chris Senior was speaking), and our discussion at the table was deeply rooted in Scripture. It pointed out the infancy of my faith and unfamiliarity with God's Word. As the years rolled on, the leader changed to Land Bridgers and then eventually to me. It has split into new tables a few times. Some men have moved away.

Bobby Norwood

I began filling in as a substitute table leader once or twice a quarter in 2011. I took over the table full time in 2013. In 2016 I became Charlie Renfroe's backup emcee. In 2017 I joined the advisory board. In 2018

I joined the board of directors and took over as the Buckhead location leader.

I stay involved because I've seen changes in my life and in the men around my table. The ministry stays focused on a very simple formula that knowing Christ and studying God's Word will make you a better husband, father, friend, boss, coworker, etc. At times, LMI has asked me to step up, and I've been honored for those opportunities.

I'll never forget when a man at my table came bounding into the restaurant with his finger stuck in his Bible. He'd read something he could not wait to share with the other men. "You guys! Check this out! Isn't this amazing?!" Those moments are the best. At the same time, going into deep, dark, scary places with men in crisis is where I feel the closest to Christ.

When I walked in, I was really young. And I'm still comparatively young. Dealing with flighty, distracted young men is hard. They're full of excuses. They need accountability. But if I start to sound like a parent, they're gone for good. It's a delicate challenge.

One of my top jobs and goals is growing new table leaders. It's hard work. Sometimes they don't want the responsibility, even though they are clearly equipped to do the task well. Patience in every aspect of life is hard, but especially with this.

Stephen O'Day, Attorney

I have been involved in FMMF about twelve years, including eight years as a table leader. I have found fellowship, fulfillment, growth, and inspiration from my weekly preparation for our table discussions and the weekly discussions. I believe it has brought more meaning and a biblical approach to my various leadership roles (professional, volunteer, family).

What I enjoy most is the personal growth I receive from my weekly prayer and preparation for our meetings. I even review and prepare during the weeks I

Stephen O'Day

cannot attend and lead, because it has such meaning for me.

207

Colin White, Former Marine Airborne Ranger, CFA

I have been involved in FMMF for about seventeen years, since I returned to Atlanta after serving in the Marine Corps. I think my dad always thought I would come home. He felt like he had broken down barriers for me, had plowed the fields, and thought I could be successful in whatever I wanted to do. I think he always believed he had forged a path that his own father never could. He could make his own way if he was called by God to serve. He was not testing God's favor, but he believed that God was testing his mettle.

Colin White

In the same way, my dad tested me. He drove me to that recruiter's office, knowing that, with my grades, I had a pretty good chance of getting a scholarship, and if I received a scholarship, it would have been impossible for me to turn it down. We didn't have a lot of money, and I wanted to test myself by attending a top-ranked school and by joining the Marine Corps.

In one sense, he didn't care what school I went to or what branch of the military I joined. At one point he had me headed to the navy after never saying one positive thing about his own military experience. He wanted me to follow in his footsteps and to think about all of these résumé builders as a means to an end. The more successful I looked, the more I could relate to a man who was broken but was putting on a front of success or wealth to mask his insecurity. He knew that men needed to know their Creator to be made whole and to be accepted into His kingdom. That's how I became a table leader.

Mike Lenhart, Location Leader, Charlotte FMMF

I started attending the Buckhead FMMF in 2012 at the invitation of my friend Beau Bearden. I had been attending church regularly in Atlanta, but I really wasn't doing much outside of my Sunday attendance. The leadership aspect of FMMF appealed to me most of all. I've always considered myself a leader. I had graduated from West Point and served in the army, but I would not have described myself as a Christian leader in the slightest sense.

Fast-forward nearly seven years since my fellowship table at the Buckhead On the Border and much has changed in my life, all for the good, and much is the result of the FMMF. I became a regular leader at my table in Atlanta. I attended regularly. And when I announced to the table that I was moving to Charlotte, Dave Dorries challenged me to start a FMMF chapter there! "What?" I thought. "I'm not ready for that!" Chris White talked to me a couple of times after I moved to Charlotte, and he encouraged me to let a chapter grow organically.

When God calls, we respond. So I did. And the Charlotte FMMF was formed in early 2015. The group is small but consistent. And much like my transformation, I have witnessed the same from the men who attend regularly in Charlotte.

So what has FMMF meant to me? I'm confident and comfortable in my Christian principles, and I'm comfortable in engaging men and women in Christian dialog at work and in social settings. In a short amount of time since moving to Charlotte, I have become an elder at Myers Park Presbyterian Church. I lead a Wednesday early morning run group that huddles in prayer during our cooldown, and I write a devotional blog a couple of times a month. All of these activities point directly back to my involvement with FMMF.

Leadership Ministries has provided me with tools and given me the moral courage to execute to a high degree in my community. I am beyond grateful!

Daniel DeCriscio, Location Leader, Atlanta, Grant Park FMMF

In 2012, a pastor-in-residency at our church invited me to attend the Buckhead FMMF. I wasn't really looking for a men's discipleship group at the time, as I was already involved in a couple of groups at my church. I also wasn't sure if I fit in, as I'm not in real estate and don't play golf! But I found something at On the Border that was really special and compelling. Every Friday there was a gospel message that zeroed in on the unique challenges of being a man, and a humble group of men encouraged one another in faith and repentance. These men were, as Dan Allender said, "leading with a limp." It was unique, attractive, and I couldn't stop coming back.

Fast-forward five years, our family moved into an underserved Atlanta neighborhood with the mission of building friendships and finding ways to serve. In meeting many Christians already in the neighborhood, I noticed a shared vision and passion for racial reconciliation, men's discipleship, and community, but we weren't doing life together. Our own church relationships, affiliations, and programs had us in silos. I shared this in passing to Chris White Jr. one day, and without any hesitation he blurted out, "Why don't you plant a Friday Morning Men's Fellowship in Grant Park?"

Daniel DeCriscio

At first I thought this was crazy, but as I reflected and prayed, the Holy Spirit showed me the need seemed to match with the offering and the opportunity. God put a small group of ethnically diverse men in my midst whom I saw as pioneering leaders. We started meeting, praying, and hanging out together in the summer of 2017 with no expectations. We are hopeful that by abiding as brothers in Christ we'll be equipped to disciple one another into "acting in line with the truth of the gospel," as Paul said in Galatians 2, breaking down barriers and being better neighbors, husbands, fathers, and leaders.

My wife has noted that this pursuit "has been a blessing to Dan and our family. It has given Dan a community of men to lean on and grow in his faith and as a leader." We even launched a chapter of the Unite Network out of this group, which seeks to promote oneness and human flourishing across socioeconomic and denominational barriers.

But this endeavor is not without its challenges. In a community like mine, there's a lack of trust, and people are quite skeptical of newcomers with big ideas. It's easy for me to get discouraged when I see potential leaders or newcomers to the faith choose not to commit to the group. Sometimes I take it personally, but then I remember that the success of this group is driven by our faithfulness to God and one another and the Holy Spirit. It's not about me, and it's not about a program. It's about Jesus and the men He's drawn to us in our particular context.

And I also see what God has done through Chris Sr. and the Buckhead group. When you see the vibrancy of that group, it can be intimidating and cause you to ask, "What's our small little group doing wrong?" But then I remember that group was built over thirty-five years of faithful, humble men pursuing one another and the Lord. And we pray for and hope for the same in Grant Park.

Savannah Boyd, Wife of Brian Boyd

I'm sure many men have wondered at one time or another if the time they invest in FMMF is worth it. I'm here to tell you that, yes, it is. It directly impacts your peers, your colleagues, your family, your children, and your wife. FMMF is providing a place where my husband can engage in critical fellowship. Brian receives biblical encouragement to become the kind of husband and father he wants to be.

Brian has always had a strong footing in the Lord. In fact, we just celebrated our eighth wedding anniversary. I remember while we were engaged there was some family drama—something crazy and silly on my side of the family—and as we worked our way through it, I wondered why Brian would want to marry into that. When I asked him, he said, "Just as Christ has unconditional love for you, so do I. My love is not based on a condition that your family is perfect or you are perfect. My love for you is unconditional."

Men, your wife needs to know that from you and believe it at her core. FMMF challenges my husband, Brian, in such a way that I can genuinely rest in that promise. I think this kind of measure of men's character is the ultimate testimony to how FMMF is accomplishing its mission. Don't ever underestimate the influence you have on one another. We are all products of the company we keep. I am forever grateful for the impressions that many of you have made on my husband. I'm humbled to be Brian's wife, and I'm eternally grateful for the part FMMF has played in Brian becoming the man he is today.

Brian Boyd, Atlanta Real Estate Professional, FMMF Table Leader

The main reason I have stayed involved is accountability. Having a group of men who are in the same stage of life who can relate to things I am going through and provide encouragement is a real blessing. It's rare to have this as a man in our society today, and I wish it was more prevalent. I have become a better leader to my friends outside of FMMF and, most important, within my home. When my wife tells me that she sees the difference in me from FMMF, that is all the reason I need to stay actively involved.

I enjoy my role as a table leader, I enjoy helping with the annual fund-raiser. I know it is vital to the ministry, and giving back with my time and ideas is gratifying and enjoyable. I like working behind the scenes to make things happen, especially for such a great cause.

Sean Dacey, Table Leader, On the Border, Atlanta FMMF

I first came to FMMF in February 2010. I became a table leader in the beginning of 2013. I shared my story and I have been a speaker at FMMF and volunteered at the charity golf tournament. I was part of the first Leadership Ministries–sponsored Radical Mentoring and also did Radical Mentoring 2.0. I was initially drawn to FMMF, after my introduction to Jeff Terry, by the transparency and fellowship of the men at the table and the comfortable feel of the format.

Sean Dacey

What's kept me involved is not only the men and the friendships I've developed, who have helped me on the path, but also the incredible impact it's had on my marriage, my family life, and my interactions at work.

FMMF gave me a different perspective on what leadership means. Before my involvement with FMMF, I had a challenge connecting my spiritual life to my leadership responsibilities. But through my involvement that path became clearer, first by listening and experiencing the stories and actions of other men involved, and then by becoming one of those men. First in my family, at work, and now in my community. I enjoy the table fellowship. Iron sharpening iron. We are constantly being renewed. It never seems to fail that someone at the table has just what the other one needs in challenged times.

My biggest challenges are staying connected with the group and those men who come less frequently. The FMMF time commitment is not too time consuming. At the beginning, I thought my initial table members would be together forever. But life happens, people move away, take different jobs, have family commitments that become a conflict. Riding the ebbs and flows while still keeping everyone connected, finding ways for myself and my table to be more connected with other members continues to be a regular challenge for me.

Cheryl Dacey, Wife of Sean Dacey

Six years ago we were living the fast-paced rat race of everyday life. I used to describe it as feeling like a hamster on a wheel going in circles and playing beat the clock all day. What made it more challenging was that Sean and I weren't on the same hamster wheel. Following the economic downturn of 2007–2009, we found ourselves unexpectedly juggling two full-time jobs, three businesses, and two small children. Additionally, we were working through the recent illness and death of Sean's father, which impacted Sean greatly. He was struggling to cope.

The good news is we were committed partners with "I'll do whatever it takes" attitudes. The bad news is that left us without boundaries or clear lines of responsibility, which left us stressed and overwhelmed, with empty tanks and nothing left over for each other at the end of the day. The tail was definitely wagging the dog, and we were slowly growing apart.

Thankfully a board member of Leadership Ministries, Jeff Terry, entered the scene. I was working for Jeff at Peachtree Tents and Events. On numerous occasions, I noticed that Jeff would quarantine himself in his office every Thursday. Jeff openly spoke of his involvement in a men's fellowship group, so I felt comfortable asking him, "What is it that you do on Friday mornings that requires so much thought and preparation?" The time he was spending in solitude was allowing him to prepare his weekly message on the study at the table he would lead the next morning. He shared that the group had been instrumental in turning his life around. It had made a huge impact on his personal and professional life when he made the decision to follow Christ.

Jeff asked me if he could invite Sean. When Sean accepted his invitation, I knew it was an answer to my prayers. Sean came home that Friday morning, and I knew I saw a different man standing in front of me. Sean said he loved it and definitely wanted to go back again. I was very excited. He continued to go back week after week and has seldom missed a Friday morning over the past six years. He found the connection he was missing with a group of like-minded men who were being held accountable to Christ. He found a safe environment to share his struggles and learn from the struggles of other men. Sean found a place where he could excel as a man, a father, and a husband. He was excited and started to dream again and have hope and faith. He was ready to change the world!

Sean's passion was recognized by leaders like Jeff, Dave Dorries, and Chris White, who were able to channel, foster, and steer his focus from one of saving the world to saving his family and marriage first. And it has worked! Now he shows gratitude for the little things that helped to foster more intimacy in our marriage. Sean has advanced to become a table leader and speaker at FMMF. I'm certain he has impacted many of the men at his table positively and is a role model for me and our children and an inspiration to many friends and family. We are committed to each other, our faith, and our family. We are works in progress. I am truly humbled and forever grateful for the gift of FMMF.

Matt Lacey, Table Leader, Atlanta, Perimeter FMMF

Chris White trained me as a table leader twelve years ago, and it has changed my life forever. The 3P method used in the FMMF keeps me organized as I lead my table weekly. It helps me ensure that I stay focused on the main point, and therefore the men at my table are also able to get the main point. The icebreaker is something I use in multiple areas of my life: at dinners with friends at home, meeting strangers, or talking with family. The icebreakers allow everyone at the table to participate, and so no one feels left out. The application makes sure that, as a table leader, I help the participants to apply biblical principles to their everyday lives.

The best part about being trained by Chris is that he is tough with high standards and expectations. Because Chris loves me, he taught me to follow Christ's example to lead the table well. I have seen exponential spiritual growth in several men at my table. Their spiritual growth was made possible because Chris White poured himself into my training as a table leader.

Katy Lacey, Wife of Matt Lacey

I have been married to Matt for five years, and he has led a table for twelve years. My heart has been nurtured and our relationship strengthened because Matt pours himself in a Christlike manner into the men at his FMMF table. It was his spiritual growth that attracted me to him in the first place. He is disciplined in his study of the Bible, and he is a godly husband to me as a result.

Matt often brings elements of his table leading into our home dinner parties with his thoughtful icebreakers. For example, the guests at our dinner parties love to come because Matt and I are welcoming and they feel listened to. Our home is more hospitable now than it has ever been because Matt has been trained by the FMMF to be a leader in his marriage, our family, and his business.

Andrew Day, Table Leader, Atlanta, On the Border FMMF

I have been attending Friday mornings for over eight years, and the meetings have been instrumental in helping me develop a deeper, more personal relationship with Jesus Christ. After I met my wife, I had a desire to renew my walk as a Christian man, but I didn't know where to start. I had turned my back on the church and Jesus for the better part of a decade as I went off to college and started my professional career in New York.

Andrew Day

My dad and brother-in-law encouraged me to join them at FMMF, and I was connected to Christopher White and Alec Dicks's table. I immediately saw a group of guys who were doing life together: studying the Word of God and sharing the struggles and challenges they were facing as husbands, fathers, leaders in their respective businesses, and life in general. It was a refreshing perspective that was led by a desire to know Jesus better, and it opened the veil that I was not the only one facing similar challenges.

In 2012, I signed up for the inaugural Radical Mentoring program that was a deep dive into Christianity for a year, led by Bob Voyles and Alan Bullock. I created lasting bonds with the five guys in my cohort and deepened my knowledge and faith of Christianity.

At the thirtieth anniversary celebration of LMI, I was chosen to speak about my experience of Radical Mentoring and how it was shaping and impacting my marriage and walk with Christ. In summation, I told the crowded banquet hall that nothing replaces personal quiet time with our Lord and Savior. "Practice doesn't make perfect, it makes permanent."

Following that short speaking opportunity, I approached Chris and told him I wanted to become a regular speaker and asked if he would coach and mentor me. I started with my testimony and then was given the opportunity to bring a message. Chris and I met for breakfast and discussed the depth of the scripture I was speaking on, and then I presented it to a small group in the LMI offices as a dry run. I embraced the process that Chris diligently guided me through and developed a special relationship with him during this preparation that I have carried forward over my first five or six messages.

I've delivered a number of messages at On the Border, and every time I dive below the surface of the scripture and learn that it's much more profound and impactful than our mind's original first interpretation. The speaker certainly gets more from the message than anyone else. It's truly an honor and privilege to share God's Word with a group of men who are in different phases of their individual walks.

FMMF has been instrumental in helping me deepen my personal relationship with Christ. And I have developed relationships and friendships with the men at my table who I would not have otherwise met. It has challenged me to be a better husband, father, leader, and friend, all by leading with Jesus. It has set me on a trajectory where I'm now impacting the next generation by teaching my two girls the meaning and importance of a life that is dedicated to Jesus.

I am a Friday morning guy and will always be a Friday morning guy.

Here are several stories from a number of people who have been involved with Leadership Development Company programs and services.

Danny R. Frances, CEO, Legacy Health Services Inc.

It is with great pleasure and much deep appreciation that I submit a brief summary of the impact Chris White and Leadership Development Company, combined, have had on my career, personal life, and my marriage and family life as well.

I was referred to Chris White in 2007 by a friend and advisor John Dodd upon my retirement and the sale of my companies. It was a time in my life when I sensed a great need to make sure of who I am, where I was going, and how I was going to get there. When you retire, or should I say step back to take a break, a person begins to ask real probing questions about life.

My first consult with Chris was introductory but meaningful enough that I came back. In 2007 I was fifty-six years old and had accomplished most everything I had set as goals in my life. My family thought it was crazy to go to Atlanta and engage a firm to help me clarify where I was going or what I wanted to do. Chris did not mince words with me, but he began to reveal to me the possibilities available when a man really knows who he is and where he is going in life.

I always wanted to know myself and my limitations better, and when all the testing was done, it was very revealing.

Danny Frances

Now it is important to state right here that my wife, Sherry, accompanied me during this testing and was very much a part of the process. When we actually sat down to review the results of all of that testing, she was in total agreement with much of it. I was very surprised. In fact, when I told her I was writing this for Chris, I asked her what impact it had for her when we went through it. She told me that while it confirmed a lot for her about me, it also helped her understand the man I was designed to be.

My faith in Jesus Christ has always been an integral part of my life, but this testing and review with Chris over my testing results solidified my heart purpose in life to serve the Lord. It is in the marketplace where I am designed to be and to impact people for him. It was no coincidence that, by the end of 2008, I was already in business again, but this time with my youngest son. We have now grown our company, and I do not intend to retire again. I was even better prepared to mentor my son and other key people in our organization.

Lastly, the time has gone by quickly since 2007, when I first met Chris, but I have remained in contact with him and LDC and would encourage others to go through that process. Leadership Development and Chris have forever impacted my life, the way I now do business, and enhanced my marriage and family life. Chris is my friend today as well.

Thomas E. "Trey" Lucy III, Real Estate Broker, Charleston, South Carolina

I want you to know how much I appreciate the work you have done with me over the past twelve years. We began working together when I was a junior in high school, and your guidance through the Life and Career Planning process has benefited my life in so many ways. It helped me with college selection and the focus of my studies, it gave me a strategic advantage in successfully finding employment, and it is currently helping me succeed in a very competitive environment.

Trey Lucy and family

The program has been successful for me because it empowered me to realize some of my goals and aspirations based on the assessment of my innate abilities and aptitudes. The beauty to me of the Life and Career Planning process is that it teaches each individual about themselves, their own inner potential and uniqueness.

At an early age I realized through the planning process and your counsel that I did not want to just flounder around, but that I could learn about myself and make informed and educated choices in my life's path rather than end up in middle age wishing I had done something else with my life.

Chris, along with the tools used in the program, your personal knowledge of the business world and your life experiences have given you a unique perspective to listen, make assessments, and then help a person think through any given situation, based on this knowledge of themselves and their own internal compasses. This, in turn, helps them to make wise, educated decisions.

Lt. Col. James Edward "Jed" Sorenson, U.S. Army (Retired)

When I met you, Chris, in the autumn of 2007, I was nine months from retiring after twenty years in the army, and I did not have a clue what I should do with the rest of my life. The only answer I could give to the question "What do you want to do?" was "The best I can in whatever job I get." As I approach the first anniversary of my new career, I want to report to you how your influence made the difference.

First, the personal interest you showed from the beginning and through-out the three-month process put me at ease, allowing you to really under-stand who I am, even better than some of my closest friends. You challenged me to discover who God created me to be while also building me up and encouraging me by pointing out the strengths I have that I had previous-ly not considered. Most important, you counseled me concerning how my God-given aptitudes and skills were valuable and that I had much more to offer a prospective employer than I was able to communicate. You helped me develop the confidence and ability to communicate these strengths.

Specifically, through your mentorship, you enabled me to commu-nicate much more effectively about who I am. I was also able to create a refined résumé that led to my current position. Now I am in a job that challenges me, is filled with opportunity, surrounds me with people I enjoy working with, and provides for my family.

Chris, I am convinced you are doing what God has put you here to do. I give Him credit for using you as a tool to help me make the transition from a successful career in the army to a new career that, because of your help, is the right career for me now. Thank you for being a good steward of the gifts God has given you.

Harold Fickett, Prominent Literary Figure and Chuck Colson's Ghostwriter for Many Years, and Creator of Scenes Media Website

I recently spent some time cleaning up my office, and I came upon the in-struments we used in our Life and Ca reer Planning sessions together. I was reminded again of how invaluable this experience has proved. I realized in the past few years, rather late in life, I experienced a more profound sense of being lost in my vocation than I had ever known before. My confidence was wiped out. This had not only psycho-

Harold Fickett

logical and spiritual effects but physical ones as well, as the high level of stress produced chronic fatigue.

The process we worked through together, along with your personalized attention and training, taught me how to recapture those things about myself I have always liked, plus added several crucial pieces of knowledge about things I didn't know or understand. These latter insights help me to see around my own corners and respond to difficult situations more astutely.

For instance, I always thought I had a melancholy temperament, with inexplicable highs and lows. The testing you did revealed that I have a choleric temperament, and the lows (as well as many conflicts in my life) come about because I get profoundly angry. That was hard for me to recognize, because I'm not a typical hothead with a short fuse. I have a long, long fuse. Once ignited, though, the subsequent explosions, however long in coming, lead in destructive directions. So I have learned to remind myself constantly that anger doesn't work for me and to rely on circuit breakers—letting time pass, praying about the problem—before responding and making a bad situation worse. I've also learned how to build a team with people who have talents different from my own.

The most powerful thing I would say about the training, though, is the confidence it provides. I remember you talking about learning to "wear" the insights I've gained, meaning letting this knowledge become second nature. Now, in any given situation, I'm able to say, "This is who I am. I know how I was made and the tasks I can most easily accomplish, as well as those that are more difficult and some where I really should rely on others' help. So I can do this, or if I want to do this, I had better build a team to help me."

I used to wonder why I had often been in situations where I was starting an organization or a project from scratch. Why was there always a mountain to climb? I discovered that God made me for such tasks. I'm better able to cope with the indefinite than most. Providence and the natural order work together. God has given me both a relish for what others might think impossible and challenges along this line. The difficulties, however difficult, have really been a blessing, because otherwise I would have been bored to tears.

My work with you, Chris, has prepared me to finish strong in a race that's closer to the end than it used to be. I might have wandered off into a corner, but instead, I found my niche! Thank you.

Sophie Newsom, Davidson College Graduate, After Getting Her First Job

Here are some of the things I have learned in the job search process: I become more comfortable with uncertainty, taking things one step at a time, and trusting that my persistence will eventually pay off. Each temporary job or internship I had provided valuable experience and grew my confidence, whether I enjoyed the role or not. I became more familiar with business environment, culture, behavior, communication.

My mom often reminded me, and I believe this is true, that the longer it takes to find a job, the more you appreciate the job when you have it. Leadership Development Company helped me in my search in so many ways. Here are some of the ways that come to mind:

1. The Life and Career Planning process gave me greater self-awareness. Through the various assessments of temperament, motivation, values and aptitude, it was so helpful to get a full (personality, skills, etc.) picture of myself. It is so valuable to gain an understanding of yourself, your strengths and weaknesses, what environments are suited for you or not, so that you can find your niche and be the happiest, healthiest, most effective, and energized.

2. It was invaluable to have an objective sounding board, judge, mentor who could draw me out and with whom I could talk things out. Having someone to help me see the possibilities I had not seen was so helpful. Suzanne really helped me.

3. LDC gave me interview (job, networking, information) skills and helped me to secure interviews.

4. Doing all of this from a faith perspective made all of this so much more realistic and real.

———————

One day I stood outside our home on Dogwood Valley Drive, and I had another one of those *sursum corda* moments.

I lifted my heart to God.

Lord, the shingles on the roof are curling up from old age and heat. There are several leaks in the roof. Lord, help me please.

I had no idea what the Lord was going to do in response to my prayer. He had more in mind than just a new roof.

———————

Special Thanks/Teamwork

In the late 1990s, Suzanne and I had been at this work in one form or another for twenty years. Together, we had successfully launched a special ministry to men. We had helped two boys, Christopher and Colin, through college, and our youngest son, Josh, was in a good high school. Suzanne had sacrificed, scrimped, and saved whatever she could to get us to this point in life. It was time for the Lord to show Suzanne that he had not forgotten her.

One day I stood outside our home on Dogwood Valley Drive, and I had another one of those *sursum corda* moments. I lifted my heart to God. Lord, the shingles on the roof are curling up from old age and heat. There are several leaks in the roof. Lord, help me please. I had no idea what the Lord was going to do in response to my prayer. He had more in mind than just a new roof.

At about the same time, Chip Knuth, a single guy in his twenties, was just starting his career as an architect. Suzanne and I started to meet with Chip at our house for pizza on Friday nights. We had great fun dreaming and sketching together. One thing led to another, and Chip gave us a master plan for making some architectural changes to this tired split-level house. The plan would give the house new life.

Russ Neal and his partner, Mike Loia, used their construction company, Neal-Loia, to help us get started. Greg Reszutek volunteered the structural engineering work. We put on a new roof and did the framing in accordance with Chip's design. That was all we needed to launch a wonderfully fulfilling two-year experience of teamwork.

Ken Bass and I did all the demolition. His brother Jeff did the electrical work. Sandy Sanford performed his magic with some key masonry projects. Richard Owens gave us a landscape design. John Keeble bought us some hardwood flooring. Charlie Renfroe contributed the air-conditioning, John Wolfe—the insulation, Mason Zimmerman—a French door, and Ken Thrasher—a fireplace.

For two years I spent every spare moment in the new space, which had been the carport. As the general contractor, I was able to take advantage of skills I had learned, going all the way back to when I was teenager working on my mother's house. This project and the teamwork that made it all happen, is one of the greatest blessings of my life.

Suzanne, for the rest of her life on this earth, thanked God for this material provision. It meant everything to her, and she used her home generously to reach out to others.

From this rough start, a group of men added living space in our former carport and built additional space in the back yard.

From top: Sandy Sanford and Joe Pleasants working on the front; my son Josh lends a hand; Ken Bass and his wife helped with demolition; Jeff Bass handles electrical work; architect Chip Knuth and Joe Pleasants transform our home.

Our finished home on Dogwood Valley Drive was used for ministry and continues to be a great blessing to the White family.

Acknowledgments

I started this writing project (my friend Glen Jackson—co-founder of Jackson Spalding Communications, an award-winning public relations and marketing agency—told me to use that term to take the pressure off publishing a book and rather focus on the story) when I stepped down from my position at the Leadership Companies at the end of 2017. My motive was to tell the story of how so many people contributed to Suzanne's and my success in our lives and career. And I want to say thank you to them all. I have mentioned many of these people in these pages, but not all. Of course, it would take many, many more pages for that.

Don McKee, a local journalist, helped me get the story down initially. Several board members of Leadership Companies—my son Colin, Bob Voyles, Ken Thrasher, and Mark Maynard—critiqued the original manuscript. My friend Mark DeMoss was part of that effort. It was obvious to all of them that the project needed more work. "Writing is rewriting!"

Suzanne contracted cancer in 2018 and died in 2020.

After I pulled myself together in late 2021, my friend Chuck Johnston referred me to Emily Carmain, a veteran editor. Emily was gracious enough to postpone her retirement to help me with the rewriting, reorganizing, and expanding process. She provided the professional, critical sounding board I needed to get the story out. Always in a friendly tone, we fought over every word. She was never afraid to say no, but she was always friendly and encouraging. I thoroughly enjoyed going through the writing process with this dear woman.

Ida Bell, a friend and fellow disciple, agreed to proofread the manuscript and helped us avoid several embarrassing blunders.

Glen Jackson reentered the picture in the summer of 2022 by inviting me to breakfast. I had no idea what he had in mind. He totally surprised me when he said, "Chris, I want to help you publish your book." Glen then mobilized all the professional resources necessary to push the writing project forward.

Gene Mason, Vice President of Operations at Leadership Ministries Inc., a graphic designer as well as a writer, took the final manuscript, which was edited by Ed Curtis, and made this book. We, all of us, offer it to you for your enjoyment, encouragement, and edification.

Thank you, everyone.
Chris White
October 2022

chris.white@leadership-companies.com